My Lord Loves a Pure Heart

ACKNOWLEDGMENTS

Grateful appreciation goes to Marilyn Goldin for preparing the talks for publication, to Hemananda for invaluable editorial assistance, to Diane Fast for copyediting, to Ed Levy, Patricia Kaiser and Christina Richardson for checking and proofreading the text, to Cheryl Crawford for design, Steve Batliner for design and typesetting, Leesa Stanion for assistance on the glossary, Judith Levi for assistance on compiling the index and Rowena Kemp for overseeing production of this book.

— *Swami Kripananda*

First published 1994.

05 04 03 02   6 5 4 3

Printed in the United States of America

Chidvilasananda, Swami
My Lord loves a pure heart / Swami Chidvilasananda.
p. cm.
Includes index.
ISBN 0-911307-29-X
1. Spiritual life—Hinduism. I. Title
BL1237.36.C55 1984
294.5'4—dc20 94-14948
CIP

My Lord Loves a Pure Heart

The Yoga of Divine Virtues

Swami Chidvilasananda

A Siddha Yoga® Publication
Published by the SYDA Foundation

SWAMI CHIDVILASANANDA

In the beginning, love.

In the end, love.

In the middle,

we have to cultivate virtues.

— Swami Chidvilasananda

Contents

Note on Sanskrit Terms

All Sanskrit terms and quotations are given in a slightly modified version of the international standard system, to enable the reader to distinguish the pronunciation easily. So *ś* is written as *śh*, *ṣ* appears as *ṣh*, *c* is shown as *ch*, and the semivowel *ṛ* is written as *ṛi*.

For the convenience of the reader, well-known Sanskrit terms that come within the body of a paragraph appear as regular text. Less familiar terms are in italics with a diacritical mark to distinguish the long vowels.

Further information on Sanskrit terms in the text can be found in the Glossary, which also shows the correct pronunciation of each word. A pronunciation guide accompanies the Glossary.

Preface

In 1993, in the mountains of upstate New York, Gurumayi — as Swami Chidvilasananda is affectionately called — began delivering a remarkable series of talks around a central theme. Her subject was the magnificent virtues described in a chapter of the *Bhagavad Gītā* entitled "The Yoga of the Division Between the Divine and the Demoniacal." The setting for Gurumayi's first talk was the opening of the summer retreat, which that year coincided with the celebration of her birthday, at the Siddha Yoga meditation ashram. She returned to the subject periodically throughout the fall and winter, and all of these talks have also been included.

In Gurumayi's hands, the dust blows off the virtues and you realize how magnificent they really are. Fearlessness, respect, freedom from anger, compassion for all beings — these shining qualities, she tells us, are an integral part of our nature. They are not remote aspirations, not trophies we must struggle to attain; they are at home within us. "The point is to discover what you have already been given and learn to take care of it," she said on one occasion. Elsewhere, she remarked, "You cannot say that virtues are the ultimate goal of spiritual life. On the other hand, no one reaches the goal without them." She went on to quote one of the Desert Fathers, saying that our ultimate goal is the kingdom of God but our immediate purpose is the cultivation of virtue and a pure heart.

Perhaps this gives you some idea of the subtle clarity of Gurumayi's approach and the richness of her references. She is equally at ease with the writings of the Christian ascetics, the Sufi Masters of Islam and the poet-saints of India. It is not just that she is conversant with all these traditions and able to cite them eloquently. It is that the heart of the experience they all describe is the one in which she lives. Gurumayi's primary reference is to the Indian tradition. She quotes and expounds the loftiest, most esoteric scriptures of Vedanta and Kashmir Shaivism in a way that is so accessible and contemporary, you realize that these ancient aphorisms are about your very own life. She reintroduces you to your own greatness, to the innate goodness that exists within you.

In Sanskrit, this is known as *upadesha*, sitting close to the Truth. What true spiritual Masters give us when they speak is their own experience of the ultimate Reality. The merits of their attainment stream into their teachings. There is no form of instruction more personal than that, and paradoxically, none that is more universal.

Gurumayi concluded each one of these talks by leading people first into a contemplation of what had been said and then into meditation. This process is an intrinsic part of what she teaches. It is also the way that spiritual knowledge has always been transmitted. Once you have heard the teachings, you must reflect on their meaning in silence, to distill the essence of what has been given. Then you must imbibe it. Through the practice of meditation, you must discover it in yourself, for yourself.

After meditation, at the end of each evening program that summer, Gurumayi gave darshan. This is the time when everyone has a chance to come forward and spend a moment in her presence. It is an opportunity to say a few words, if you wish, to ask a question or exchange a greeting. Yet most people choose to experience that moment in silence, because Gurumayi's state is like a force field that you enter, like an ocean in which you swim.

The Sanskrit word *darshan* literally means "to see"— or "to come into the presence of one who truly sees." Sees what? The universe as a play of Consciousness, the vision of God in everyone. An encounter with such a being has the potential of awakening the knowledge that lies dormant within you, in your understanding of the world and your perception of other people. Coming into contact with a Siddha Guru makes the possibility of spiritual attainment actual, tangible, real.

How did Gurumayi become the vehicle of such tremendous power? When she was five years old, she met an extraordinary yogi, an enlightened Master named Swami Muktananda. She accepted him as her Guru, and from that moment on, his small country ashram in western India became her second home. So, from the very beginning, hers was a consecrated life.

Swami Muktananda was a classical *sannyāsin*, a renunciant who set out on a burning quest for the highest Truth at the age of fifteen. He walked from one end of India to the other, studying the ways and teachings of charismatic holy men who lived in forests and mountains, monasteries and temples. Over a period of thirty years, he accumulated a vast storehouse of knowledge. He mastered yoga and Vedanta, he memorized the esoteric poetry of the saints and acquired a host of practical skills, with the name of God always turning in his mind. But it was only when Muktananda met his own Guru, Bhagawan Nityananda, that all the years of hardship and effort bore fruit.

Bhagawan Nityananda was a born Siddha, a perfected being—one of the greatest saints and Gurus of this century. He lived beside an ancient temple in Ganeshpuri, a tiny village set in the wilderness of the Tansa valley, north of Bombay. He had mysterious ways of conferring grace. This Nityananda was an *avadhūta*, an ecstatic, unconventional being, who lived in a state beyond body-consciousness. Children adored him. He spoke very little, and what he did say was often expressed in a cryptic way. Yet he was the embodiment of the teachings and the freedom that Muktananda sought so ardently. Thousands of people loved Bhagawan Nityananda because miracles and legends sprang up like flowers wherever he walked. Muktananda loved him because Nityananda gave shaktipat, the priceless gift of the great inner awakening of the soul.

Early one morning, this astounding Siddha Master looked into Muktananda's eyes. A shaft of golden light in his gaze awakened the power of Kundalini Shakti, the divine energy, at the core of Muktananda's being. This was shaktipat, the rarest and most profound of all initiations. All at once, the bliss that Muktananda had sought for years and years was placed within his reach and the grace of an ancient lineage of sages, seers, and saints poured into him.

SWAMI MUKTANANDA

During the next nine years, Muktananda meditated in seclusion with startling intensity, letting the energy that had been awakened in him unfold in its entirety. Then, one quiet afternoon, Bhagawan Nityananda suddenly began to dance. He told the people around him that Muktananda had attained liberation. Though, physically, they were hundreds of miles apart, the Guru and his disciple had become one. Shortly afterward, Nityananda called him back to Ganeshpuri to live.

For the rest of Bhagawan Nityananda's days, Swami Muktananda tried to veil his attainment. Yet, despite this, many began to see in him the living example of what Nityananda really had to give. Then, just before he died, Bhagawan Nityananda called Muktananda to his side and passed on to him the authority and mystical power of his lineage. He told Muktananda that one day he was to carry the grace-bestowing power of the Siddhas to the rest of the world. It is rare indeed for even such a consummate yogi to become established in the experience of the supreme Self, to attain liberation. But to dispense the grace of centuries of enlightened Masters, to be a Siddha Guru and sit on that seat of power, is something even more than that.

This was the period in which Gurumayi first came to Ganeshpuri as a child and met her Guru. She grew up spending all her weekends and holidays in his ashram. When she was in her early teens, he gave her shaktipat, the great initiation that Bhagawan Nityananda had given him, and she stepped into the mystical realm of Muktananda's world. Shaktipat ignited in her the same deep longing for the highest Truth that had characterized Baba Muktananda's own spiritual practice. Meditation became the focus of her life. Even though she went to school during the week, her heart was set on becoming a yogini, a renunciant like Baba.

As she was growing up, Baba Muktananda's mission was also growing. He was becoming a world teacher. First, seekers from many different countries began to find their way to his ashram. Then, true to his Guru's command, Muktananda himself began to travel. At a time when everyone was talking about political, social, and cultural revolution, Muktananda brought what he called his "meditation revolution" to the West. He brought shaktipat, he brought chanting and all the treasures of yoga. Muktananda's attainment was so unshakable that he was able to synthesize all his years of study and practice into a path that contained the cream of the Indian tradition, the crown jewels of yoga. Before long, Gurumayi was asked to accompany his tour.

When she was a shy teenager of nineteen, Muktananda made her his translator, even though she spoke halting English at the time. This grew to mean that every word he communicated to the thousands of people who came to see him, all the teachings he delivered on two world tours, all his advice and solace and insight went through her. His instructions, his perceptions, his thoughts were constantly moving through her mind.

As the years passed, Muktananda gave her more and more responsibility. "Yoga is skill in action," says the *Bhagavad Gītā,* and that is what you thought of when you saw her working. Gurumayi had a very public role to fulfill, even in those days. At the same time, she was actively engaged in a classical interior sadhana — meditation, chanting, studying the scriptures, serving the Master. She sustained this sadhana wherever Baba's tour went, in the midst and in front of thousands of other seekers. Within the context of her own life, amidst the fabric of life in the ashram and while touring the world, she gave herself to the mysterious alchemy of the Guru's grace with a fire and a purity of purpose that took your breath away.

Gurumayi's whole life has always been about following the Guru's command, which she does impeccably and to the letter. Of all the elements of the Guru-disciple relationship, this is perhaps the most crucial, the most fruitful, and the most difficult one to achieve. Muktananda used to say, "Powers or realizations are not things that descend from the blue sky and enter us. Powers and realizations are achieved through obedience to the Guru's command." Gurumayi always took this statement literally, with the understanding that it held the key to all attainments. She allowed it to shape her and prepare her to receive what her Guru wanted to give her. Whenever Muktananda gave her a command, whether simple or complex, she carried it out immediately, wholeheartedly, without modifying it or cutting any corners.

In the course of time, she came to imbibe every aspect of the accomplishment of this renowned Siddha Master. His wisdom, his

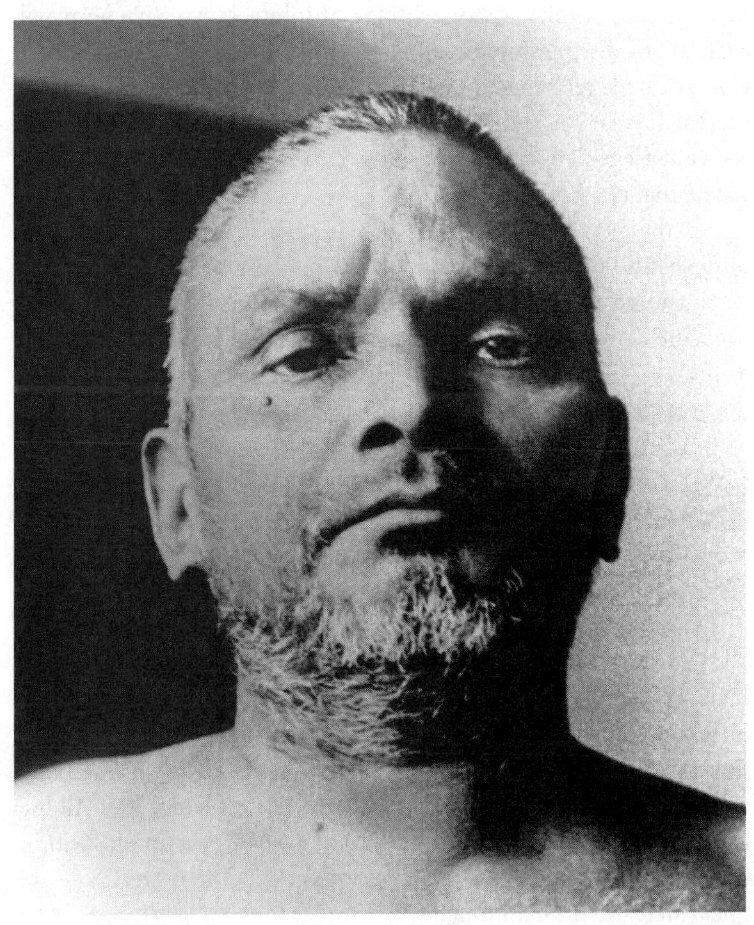

BHAGAWAN NITYANANDA

practical acumen, his compassion and his selflessness, his knowledge of medicine, cooking, scriptures, music, and the ways of the heart—all this she attained. Finally, Muktananda instilled in her the all-consuming power of his state, which the yogis call *sahaja samādhi*, waking meditation, unbroken union with the Absolute. It was a phenomenal example of discipleship, indelible proof that the teachings and the Guru-disciple relationship can set one free, that the goal of spiritual life, call it what you will — Self-realization, enlightenment, liberation — is not a legend from a bygone time but a reality that is within reach, a state that can be attained.

At the moment of shaktipat, the Guru sows a precious seed. The disciple must protect it and nourish it with his own self-effort. It is his responsibility to care for it as it sprouts into a tender plant. At the same time, the Guru continuously bestows the grace to sustain it and guide its growth. Gradually, over the years, the young sapling matures into the great tree of enlightenment.

In 1982, five months before Muktananda passed away, Gurumayi took the vows of monkhood. Her Guru gave her the name Swami Chidvilasananda, which means "the bliss of the play of Consciousness." A few days later, he installed her on the Siddha Guru's seat. Now the lineage of Masters speaks through her.

Muktananda's Siddha Yoga is what she lives and what she teaches. She has called Siddha Yoga meditation the inner journey to the heart. It is a pilgrimage that begins with shaktipat, the descent of grace. This initiation is the dawn of sadhana, of spiritual life. As a result, meditation arises spontaneously, our interest and appetite for spiritual discipline quickens, and the quest for liberation gets under way. All the branches of yoga become a natural part of the path that unfolds within us. The virtues — our divine inheritance, our inner wealth — are unearthed and brought to light.

Each of the virtues that Gurumayi discusses in this book is a profound discipline, and each one, practiced sincerely, takes a seeker to the same state of inner stillness, the experience of the Self. This is the place Gurumayi speaks from. It is one of the reasons why the virtues come to life in her presence and in her teachings. She puts us in touch with the same purity inside us. Whether the source of this purity is referred to as the Self, Consciousness, the Lord, or the goddess Kundalini—whether it is called "He" or "She" or "It"—Gurumayi is pointing to something which is beyond language. In the same way, her stories, her anecdotes and her quotations may refer to "he," "she," "it," or "them." Whatever the pronoun, she is addressing each one of us, regardless of age or gender or culture. Gurumayi welcomes everyone to the threshold of spiritual experience. She opens the door to the realm of the heart and reveals the mystery concealed within it—the flame of Consciousness, divine and imperishable, the pure eternal Self. This is who you truly are. As you read her words, make this knowledge your own.

—*Swami Kripananda*

Foreword

Of all the scriptures of Hindu tradition, the *Bhagavad Gītā* has probably had the widest appeal over the longest time. Certainly, the spiritual goals it presents are full and conciliatory: bringing together several strands of early Indian philosophy, it integrates knowledge of a transcendent truth with devotion to a personal Lord. Yet the most important reason for the *Gītā's* long appeal may be reflected in its setting within the epic *Mahābhārata*. A lesson from Lord Krishna to the hero Arjuna — who is beset with doubt at fulfilling his terrible duty in battle — the *Gītā* leads through metaphysical reflection and visionary revelation to encouragement for selfless action. In offering a path of spiritual liberation through work in the world, Krishna's message has remained vital over the millennia.

From as early as the eighth century, when Shankara wrote his commentary on the *Gītā*, religious teachers have left us expositions highlighting one or another aspect of the text. Not only have all the classical schools of Vedanta offered commentaries on the *Gītā*, but modern luminaries like Mahatma Gandhi and Sri Aurobindo have also turned to it in their search for ways to integrate a spiritual vision into twentieth-century life. Indeed, of all the great Hindu scriptures, the *Gītā* may be the one most broadly pertinent to today's seekers struggling with the everyday contradictions of living in contemporary society.

The discourse of Swami Chidvilasananda offered here focuses on chapter sixteen of the *Gītā*, which elaborates the distinctions between a divine destiny and its opposite. Swami Chidvilasananda's exposition directs us toward the virtues to cultivate in spiritual life, and makes them immediate to us now. Coming from a line of teachers that has given devotees throughout the East and West practical access to a potent yoga, Swami Chidvilasananda speaks broadly and clearly, out of her own experience. Her descriptions of human foibles strike home and her remedies make sense. She thus effectively shares her realization through her thoughtful words as well as her powerful presence.

Let us contemplate what she has to tell us here.

—*Daniel Gold*
Department of Asian Studies
Cornell University

INVOCATION

Muktānandāya gurave śhiṣhya-saṃsāra-hāriṇe
Bhakta-kāryaika-dehāya namaste chit-sad-ātmane

Om namaḥ śhivāya gurave sac-chid-ānanda-mūrtaye
Niṣhprapañchāya śhāntāya nirālambāya tejase

Om saha nāvavatu saha nau bhunaktu
Saha vīryam karavāvahai
Tejasvi nāvadhītam astu mā vidviṣhāvahai

Om śhāntiḥ śhāntiḥ śhāntiḥ
Sadgurunāth Mahārāj kī Jay!

Salutations to Muktananda, the Guru,
who rescues his disciples from the cycle of birth and death,
who has assumed a body to meet the needs of his devotees,
and whose nature is consciousness and being.

Om. Salutations to the Guru, who is Shiva!
His form is being, consciousness, and bliss.
He is transcendent, calm, free from all support, and luminous.

Om. May we, Guru and disciple, be protected together.
May we enjoy the fruits of our actions together.
May we achieve strength together.
May our knowledge be full of light.
May we never have enmity for one another.

Om. Peace. Peace. Peace.
I hail the Master who has revealed the Truth to me!

In the Beginning, Love

With great respect and great love, I welcome you all with all my heart.

Exactly at this moment, ten o'clock in the morning, it is seven-thirty in the evening in Gurudev Siddha Peeth, our great ashram in India. They are also having a program, right now. Of course, we are beginning our celebration and they are concluding theirs, but, *ahh,* think of all the people who have gathered together in Ganeshpuri, in Gurudev Siddha Peeth, today.

Remember Bhagawan Nityananda's Temple, and his golden cosmic form. Think of Baba Muktananda's Samadhi Shrine, the walls covered with peacock feathers. The Samadhi Shrine is always very fragrant and always vibrating, of course, with the great energy, Baba's shakti—wonderful, tender, and strong. Wherever you walk in the Ganeshpuri ashram, you experience incredible love, and you know one thing for sure: every bit of Gurudev Siddha Peeth is imbued with the Guru's grace.

There is a tradition in Siddha Yoga that every journey begins and ends in the Temple at the feet of Bhagawan Nityananda. You go there to offer your salutations and to receive his blessings. We spent several months in India recently. Just before we left, I visited the cowshed. It is in a new spot these days on the far side of a big hill called Tapovan. If you want to get there quickly, you have to go by car. As we were driving there that day, I kept looking up at the sky. It was evening and the sky was magnificent — completely dark, covered with thick clouds heavy with rain, except for one little space in the west, just one little space that was completely golden. It was breathtaking. It was amazingly beautiful. The tops of the hills looked as though they were draped in golden light.

From the cowshed, I went to the Temple, and there was Bhagawan Nityananda sitting in his golden body. For, you know, in Ganeshpuri, the statue of Bhagawan Nityananda is a radiant gold. When I saw him that evening, my mind became completely still. I couldn't tell whether I was looking at Bhagawan Nityananda or the sky. As I stood there, it was very clear. There is no difference. He is the universe.

Then we came to South Fallsburg, and the first thing we did on arriving was go to the Temple. And there was Bhagawan Nityananda. That day, they had draped his form in shimmering golden cloth. The sky, Bhagawan Nityananda in the Temple in Ganeshpuri, and Bhagawan Nityananda in the Temple here — they were all the same. Wherever you go, the Guru is with you. All this is the play of Consciousness.

Now, here we are sitting in the Shakti Mandap, the pavilion of the great energy, in South Fallsburg. This is one of the most beautiful and powerful spots in the ashram. So many auspicious events have been celebrated here. We've held Intensives here, surrounded by the snow, and dancing *saptahs* around the fire, as well as many courses. We have meditated here in the golden light of many sunsets and chanted the *Guru Gītā* amidst many golden sunrises. We've had Vedic fire ceremonies with our learned brahmin priests. So much chanting has been done here, and you can feel it. You can hear the sound of chanting in the air.

Why have we gathered here this morning? Yes, we are celebrating a birthday, but there is another very important reason why you've come. We are here to launch the summer retreat of 1993. The beginning of every summer is always full of excitement, blessings, anticipation, curiosity, and lots of resolutions. Every summer has also had a theme, and this year, too, we have a specific goal. We are going to delve deeply into the subject of ashram dharma—just what does it mean to live in an ashram? What is the proper, dharmic way to spend time here? More specifically, we will look into the magnificent virtues. We will ask, "What virtues can I cultivate this summer?"

This seems like a very appropriate time to take a closer look at the virtues that lie hidden within us, our God-given gifts, to explore them, to cherish them, and to share them with others.

The Chinese philosopher Mencius once said, "The virtues are not poured into us, they are natural to us. Seek them and you will find them; neglect them and you will lose them."

Many people are afraid of these virtues. They are so lofty, people feel overwhelmed. They think they will never be able to achieve them. However, Mencius' statement throws a completely different light on the matter. Virtues are not something that you have to get from outside; they already exist within you. Therefore, the point is to discover what you have been given and to learn to take care of it.

For the great Indian sage Bhartrihari, virtue was a transforming force. Bhartrihari said, "O wise man, develop a regular practice of cultivating divine virtue, for it makes wicked men good, foolish men wise, enemies friendly, and invisible things visible. Divine virtue instantly turns poison into honey and bestows upon you the fruit of your actions."

So, that is what we are going to do here. We will examine and practice the teachings of the Siddhas on virtue. We will make great efforts to look deep into our hearts. We will open the treasure chest that waits for us there and explore the magnificent gems it contains.

Lasting happiness comes only when you realize God within. Bliss is yours when you experience the truth of your own nature. So it cannot be said that virtues are the ultimate goal of spiritual life. Yet, it is also true that no one ever reaches the goal without them. The magnificent virtues elevate you just as an addiction to vices drags you down.

We will take all the time we need to explore this subject. However, this morning, I would like to give you an overview of our theme from the highest perspective. Let us examine the question of virtue through the words of Lord Krishna in the *Bhagavad Gītā*. This scripture is one of the most sacred texts on yoga. In eighteen chapters Lord Krishna imparts the essence of wisdom to his disciple Arjuna. For the upliftment of all humanity, he gives the most practical advice on "The Yoga of Meditation," "The Yoga of Action," and "The Yoga of Devotion," as well as the subtlest teachings, such as "The Yoga of the Divine Glories."

Chapter sixteen of the *Bhagavad Gītā* is called "The Yoga of the Division Between the Divine and the Demoniacal." In twenty-four verses, Lord Krishna very masterfully lays the magnificent virtues before us — those qualities which are also known as our divine wealth — as well as the traits and impulses that must be discarded, that corrode virtue. Listen to the translation of the first five verses:

> The blessed Lord spoke:
>
> Fearlessness, purity of being, steadfastness in yoga and knowledge, giving, self-restraint and sacrifice, study of sacred texts, austerity, and uprightness,
>
> Nonviolence, truth, freedom from anger, renunciation, serenity, absence of slander, compassion for all beings, freedom from desire, gentleness, modesty, absence of fickleness,
>
> Vigor, forgiveness, fortitude, cleanliness of body and mind, freedom from malice, freedom from pride; these are the endowment of those born to a divine destiny, Arjuna.
>
> Hypocrisy, arrogance, pride, anger, insolence, and ignorance are the endowment of those born to a demoniacal destiny, Arjuna.
>
> The divine destiny leads to liberation; the demoniacal to bondage. But do not grieve! You are born to a divine destiny, O Arjuna. [16:1-5]

Truly, we too have a divine destiny — to be able to sit together and receive the wisdom of the Siddhas in its purest form, to be given such clear directions about how to absorb it and apply it. Together, we will make this summer great. Together, we will receive the blessings of nature in these beautiful mountains. Together, we will love God and share His bounty, and our virtues will grow brighter.

On this day, I thank the Lord for all those who have endeavored to make this a very happy birthday. Finally, before time, in time, and beyond time, I pray that I may always be grateful to my Guru, Baba Muktananda. His grace gives me sight. His grace gives me perception. His grace allows me to feel God's radiance, generosity, kindness, love, and all that the great Lord stands for. May I continually remember that without his grace, nothing is possible. I offer my salutations at the feet of Baba Muktananda as a continuous reminder to myself that my body, mind, and heart belong to him. I offer my salutations at the feet of Baba Muktananda with the awareness that without his love, there is no life.

Whom did Baba Muktananda love the most? For whom did he sacrifice his life? Whose love did he awaken in us? Who was his Beloved? Bhagawan Nityananda. Baba Muktananda loved his Guru. In the way he loved his Guru, he showed us what devotion was and how to love him.

Thank you, once again, for being who you are. Thank you, once again, for showing the love that you have in your hearts.

Thank you, once again, for celebrating the awareness that God is great. As I contemplate the billions of stars, planets, and galaxies placed so beautifully and precisely in the heavens with such wonderfully complex patterns, as I contemplate the nothingness inside the seed which gives birth to the tree, I realize, over and again, my life is in His hands. Without His grace, what are all these things? Therefore, on what you call the "happy, happy birthday," I celebrate the presence of God in my life. I welcome the invisible blessings.

Once again, I offer my salutations at the feet of Baba Muktananda. I pray that my head may never be separated from the brilliance of his feet. May all my thoughts dissolve at his compassionate feet.

With great respect and great love, I welcome you all with all my heart.

June 24, 1993

CHAPTER ONE

FEARLESSNESS

Abhayam

WITH GREAT RESPECT AND GREAT LOVE, I welcome you all with all my heart.

The most auspicious moment of your life is when you make the commitment to know the Truth, a commitment so firm there is no turning back. Of course, getting to this point is not easy. It is easy to daydream about enlightenment. It is very easy to fantasize about being a knower of the Truth, to imagine yourself becoming established in the Truth of your nature, but actually committing yourself to it is another story. Realizing the Self is the most difficult endeavor known to humanity. Why? Because there are so many things that keep a person from coming anywhere close to it.

In one of the verses of chapter sixteen of the *Bhagavad Gītā*, Lord Krishna says to Arjuna,

> *trividhaṃ narakasyedaṃ dvāraṃ nāśhanam-ātmanaḥ /*
> *kāmaḥ krodhas-tathā lobhas tasmād-etat-trayaṃ tyajet //*

> This is the threefold gate of hell,
> destructive of the Self:
> desire, anger, and greed.
> Therefore one should abandon these three. [16:21]

Greed, anger, and desire. Anger, desire, and greed—there is no particular sequence. If a desire is not fulfilled, it does lead to anger; and anger, in turn, leads to greed. On the other hand, if there is greed and it is frustrated, deprived of its objects, there is also anger. You use that anger as energy to get what you desire; you go after it at any cost. So, you see, you rarely find any one of these three items without the others, and together they tear a person's motivation to shreds. They destroy the longing for Truth. They are like spikes, constantly punching holes in your understanding, your clear conscience, your good conduct, and all your other high principles until there is nothing left. Desire, *kāma*—which can also be translated as lust—and anger and greed are the gatekeepers, the escorts that help you across the threshold of hell.

In the *Skanda Purāna* it is said:

kāmaṃ krodhaṃ cha lobham cha yo jitvā tīrthamāviśhet /
na tena kiṇchidaprāptaṃ tīrthābhigamanād bhavet //

> When a person who has conquered desire, anger, and greed enters a holy place, there is nothing that he cannot attain on his pilgrimage.

Many people ask, "How should I live in an ashram? How should I behave in a place devoted to spiritual practices?" This verse gives you a beautiful answer. Conquer these three enemies. Keep trying to master them instead of becoming their slaves. Then you will experience the power of this place immediately and the power of the Self that dwells within you.

When people hear this, there is always a question in their minds: "Can you really overcome them completely? Desire, anger, and greed?" The sages, who mastered their senses, reply with great authority, "Yes, you can overcome them completely." However, for this, it is essential to cultivate virtues. They are the best armor. Instead of letting bad habits run you into the ground, the positive strength of virtues neutralizes their effects and eventually eliminates them altogether.

The first virtue that Lord Krishna commends to Arjuna in chapter sixteen of the *Bhagavad Gītā* is fearlessness. Jnaneshwar

Maharaj, the great poet-saint of Maharashtra, while commenting on this verse, says,

> Of all the *daivī sampatti*, the divine qualities, fearlessness holds the highest place. [16:67]

Let's think about this. Isn't it true, a person commits most of his sins out of fear? Isn't it true that out of fear, a person chooses to remain limited? Isn't it true that out of fear, a person keeps everything at arm's length—even the vision of God? Isn't it true that you've often deprived yourself of great joys, out of fear? Isn't it true that out of fear, you've lost the thing that meant most to you? Isn't it true, you tell lies out of fear? And when you call somebody else a liar, isn't that out of fear, too? Would anyone lie at all if it weren't for fear?

Baba Muktananda says, "There are only two things that inspire fear. The first is that you are not aware of the divine place of fearlessness inside you. The other is that you are not aware of God's help."

Now this is a great truth. Within you there exists a divine place of fearlessness, and God's help is always available. That is why you do sadhana, spiritual practices: to get in touch with this inner space, to become aware of the grace of God. You can't just walk down the road whistling and expect to experience the place of fearlessness inside. Nor can you egotistically pick up a hornet's nest and expect God to keep you from getting stung.

Remember, your fears are very old. As soon as your body came into existence, all your limited feelings about yourself came, too. This means that the moment you were born, your sense of helplessness and your fear of the world took birth as well. People adore newborn babies. Have you ever listened to them talk? "Oh, what a beautiful baby! Look at that face! Oh, his skin is glowing, his hair is curly. Oh, look at her tiny nails. Oh, look at those tender feet. Isn't this the most beautiful baby you have ever seen!" As much as people go on, if you could look inside the baby, you would realize it is frightened. It has been pushed into the world. You can imagine the fear. Literally, you can understand its fear of suffocation, of being choked, of being thrust into an unknown place, into the air, into the light, into the noise, where there are huge people waiting to grab hold of it. Fear is right there, at the very beginning.

The whole purpose of life is to undo your impression of limitation and the fear of the world that comes with it. The whole purpose of life is to strengthen your mind, your heart, and your body so that you can experience the Truth once again. God's glory. Boundless joy. Unconditional love. True devotion, and also the great virtues that inhabit you as an integral part of your nature.

Someone once asked Baba this question: "Why in the course of sadhana does one go through periods of feeling frightened?"

Baba replied, "When you go on a journey, you come across broken roads, and you go through thick forests. In the same way, when you are on the inner journey, you come across all sorts of places. Just as there is a center of love within you, there is also a center of fear.

"Fear is the veil that falls between the individual soul and the supreme Self. As your awareness moves closer and closer to the Supreme, you experience this fear very acutely. You become terrified of letting yourself go. It is this fear which stops you from becoming one with the Lord. Sometimes a meditator gives up meditating forever because he becomes so terrified when he reaches the center of fear.

"You should watch out for this center of fear. If you can face it, you will go beyond it. Then you will become completely fearless. If you lose yourself with great courage, you will attain That. If you hold yourself back because of fear, you will lose everything."

Such a great message: "If you hold yourself back because of fear, you will lose everything." Baba Muktananda encouraged seekers to be lionhearted. By this, he meant more than becoming strong and unafraid; he also meant being open, generous, and kind. Fears nest in dark corners. They thrive in the shadows. When the magnificent virtues shine within you, fears melt away to nothing.

Fear has many, many different shades and connotations, and an endless array of reasons for existing. Fear thrives on convoluted misgivings. Many times you must have declared to yourself or others, "I'm not afraid at all!" and in the back of your mind you ask yourself, "Is that true?" Or you say boldly, "I can do it" — whatever "it" may be — "I'm strong, I'm not the least bit frightened." And inside a little voice whispers, "Are you sure?"

Of course, sometimes a person parades around as if he or she were positively fearless. However, there always seems to be something clouding such a person's perception. Do you know what it is? Another level of fear. Fear is also afraid of itself, you see. So it conceals itself in many ways. One of its hiding places is dread, for example, the dread of an upcoming event. What sort of fear is hiding behind dread? The fear of an effort you may have to make, or the fear of having to keep a promise... If you are willing to examine yourself, you will be able to pinpoint the different disguises fear takes on for you. Sometimes fear hides behind a facade of strength. A person may seem to be very honest, straightforward, forthcoming, confiding, and so on; but when you look a little deeper, you can see that these qualities are not as pure as they seem. They are not prompted by true lionheartedness. In many cases they are an attempt to cover up apprehension, dismay, and frustration, which are all different names for fear.

Truly speaking, fear can be beneficial if it is put to the right use, and completely detrimental if it is not. As a French writer once put it: "There is a virtuous fear that is the result of faith, and a vicious fear that is the product of doubt and distrust. The first leads to hope and relies on God, in whom it believes; the other inclines to despair and does not rely on God, in whom it does not believe. Persons of the one persuasion are afraid of losing God; the other sort are afraid of finding Him."

Which type of fear do you have? Are you afraid of losing God or of finding Him? Are you afraid of losing the Truth, or are you afraid to attain the Truth?

How can you tell which type of fear you are acting from? How can you be sure your behavior is not prompted by a feeble heart? How can you actually know whether the tremor in your heart is inspired by the love of God and not by fear? Self-inquiry, self-examination is the only way. It is an essential practice. In a sense, you perform all the other spiritual practices — following the daily discipline, chanting regularly, reading, meditating, performing selfless service — to make you strong enough to support true self-examination.

Now, be careful. Self-examination doesn't mean going out and sitting under a tree or keeping to yourself and cursing the whole world. Many people do this kind of self-examination regularly. They go and sit by a stream and they tell themselves, "You are good. The world is bad. You are great. The world is not giving you as much as you deserve. You are a fine person. It is so-and-so who is a wretched soul." Particularly when people's relationships break up, this sort of self-examination begins immediately: "I gave him everything. Look what he did to me!" or "She was the one woman I could have died for. If only she had given me that love." From the yogic point of view, that sort of thing doesn't qualify as self-examination.

When you truly perform self-inquiry, which is also called *ātma vichāra*, it brings you face-to-face with yourself; and for that, you need fearlessness. Fearlessness is the virtue that ultimately allows you to recognize who you really are. You are not afraid to look in the mirror.

Every being who is born on this earth is subject to some degree of fear because of destiny and because of *samskāras*, the actions and impressions that have accumulated in the past. On the other hand, every being who is born on this earth is also worthy of the highest experience, the experience that God dwells within him.

During the summer in South Fallsburg, we offer many different courses. Almost every course is designed for the same purpose: coming to know one's own Self. It isn't just intellectual wisdom that is being dispensed. What you are being offered is the experience of the supreme Self, which dwells within you. In fact, the professors, the scholars, the swamis who give these courses all speak from their own experience. They don't teach these classes to shock your brains, or to impress you intellectually, or to find glory for themselves. They speak from the depth of their own being. When you hear a teaching that is being given from someone's experience, it has the power to affect you, to purify your mind, your heart, and your body. You can actually have the experience that is being described.

Let me share with you one of the things that happened this morning. I was walking down a corridor in the ashram, and the door to one of the rooms was open. So I looked inside and I saw all these books piled up on the bed. There were many, many different stacks of books and papers. I was fascinated. I stood there for a few seconds and then I knocked on the door very gently to get the attention of the person who was occupying the room for the time being. It was one of the professors. He was stooping over, with an armful of books. He looked up when he heard the tapping, and his glasses slipped down his nose. He peered over the lenses at me, just like a true professor, and said, "Oh! Oh!"

I asked him how he was, and he was kind enough to answer. He began to tell me how he was feeling and everything that was happening in his life. As he was speaking, all of a sudden, the face of Shirdi Sai Baba appeared. When I saw it, I remembered the very same thing had happened when I was coming out of meditation this morning. Shirdi Sai Baba's face had appeared, very, very bright, brilliantly white, dazzling. He had asked me to sing the *Pādukā Āratī*, the morning prayer that is sung in the town of Shirdi, which is his place. Some of you may not have heard about Shirdi Sai Baba. He was a great saint who lived in the state of Maharashtra, India, at the turn of the century. Millions and millions of people still go to Shirdi to visit the shrine where he is buried and many of them receive incredible blessings. Just thinking about Sai Baba is enough to invoke his blessings. When he appeared in my meditation and asked me to sing this particular prayer, I was sorry to say, "I don't know it from memory." Again, Sai Baba said, "Sing it."

So, in my meditation, I began looking for the piece of paper on which this prayer should have been written. I couldn't find it anywhere. With all the activity, I brought myself out of meditation. Now, some hours later, standing in front of the professor's door, Sai Baba's face appeared again. The professor kept talking gently, politely, sweetly, and lovingly; and I continued to watch the face of Shirdi Sai Baba, which had appeared over the professor's face. Mentally, I asked Sai Baba, "Why do you keep appearing like this, today?"

And he answered, "Fearlessness. That is what I give people: fearlessness."

When the professor came to the end of his story, Sai Baba's face also disappeared. I said good-bye and walked away. Sai Baba must have known I was going to speak to you about fearlessness tonight.

The point of narrating this incident is to bring your attention to the experience that lives inside these teachers. They have immersed themselves in what they are studying. So when these professors and the swamis, the monks of Siddha Yoga, give the teachings, they aren't just speaking from the raw knowledge of a human brain but from actual experience which has been baked, which has been assimilated and understood. That's why these courses can actually strengthen your connection to your own being. You already have the practices, the understanding. You have some tools for contemplation. So when you hear the Truth, recognition takes place within.

To attain fearlessness, spiritual practices are the noblest actions you can perform. This is why, in the ashram, whenever people say they are going through a hard time, they are advised to go to the Temple, to sit before the statue of Bhagawan Nityananda and pray. They are told, "Go to the chant; allow your heart to sing the name of God. Go and meditate. Don't be so hard on yourself. Give yourself some time."

Spiritual practices weaken the hold fear has on your mind and strengthen the love of God. They weaken the agitation of the mind and strengthen its power to be still. Spiritual practices weaken the outgoing tendencies of the senses and strengthen the longing for Truth. Of course, to gather all this fruit, you must be persevering. As the ancient sage and poet Bhartrihari said in a verse of the *Nīti Shataka*:

prārabhyate na khalu vighnabhayena nīchaiḥ
prārabhya vighnavihatā viramanti madhyāḥ /
vighnaih punaḥ punarapi pratihanyamānāḥ
prārabdhamuttamajanā na parityajanti //

> For fear of obstacles, low-spirited people do not begin anything at all. Ordinary people begin things but stop when the first difficulties arise. But the best of men, though repeatedly felled by adversities, do not abandon a noble undertaking. [27]

There are few rewards on the spiritual path as satisfying as attaining fearlessness. Once you overcome fear, the foreboding enemy, light shines through the forest of the world. Understand, what we are talking about here is overcoming the deep-seated fear which separates you from God's love.

Of course, there are also ordinary fears. For example, if you are teetering at the edge of a cliff, you experience the fear of falling. Now that is a good, healthy fear. If you're cooking and the fire is burning very high, your fingers have a fear: they don't want to go too close. Another good, healthy fear. Hang on to it. Don't misunderstand; overcoming fear does not mean getting rid of the reflexes of the body. Those reflexes are necessary. If you're walking down a muddy country road and there is a huge pothole and your foot stops, all on its own, don't say "I am unafraid" and blunder on. Pay attention to these good and reasonable fears. They are not what we are talking about at all.

We are talking about the veil that falls between the individual soul and the supreme Self, the fear that separates you from God. A poet-saint named Krishnasuta, who lived in Maharashtra in the nineteenth century, wrote a very beautiful *bhajan*, a devotional song, about fear, which says:

> What fear could exist for one whose mind is dissolved
> in the bliss of divine Consciousness?
>
> Fear arises only out of the feeling of individual existence
> Which comes from identifying with the body.
> It does not survive in the state of divine Consciousness;
> It becomes unreal even in the ordinary world then.
> The moment I realized that I was Truth, Existence, and Bliss,
> both my sins and my merits disappeared.
> The fear that death will take away his children, his wife,
> or himself

No longer bothers a man when his basic ignorance
Of identification with the body
And attachment to material wealth and family
    disappears.

The Vedas repeatedly declare that all doubts dissolve
When you realize the highest Truth, the divine Consciousness.
Krishnasuta has caught hold of the Guru's feet
Only after realizing this Truth.

In all the scriptures the sages urge us to develop a brave spirit and a courageous heart. This is another way of talking about the state of fearlessness. To attain this state, take hold of the mantra. Repeat the mantra at all costs. Attune your mind, body, and heart to the vibrations of the mantra, and let it dissolve your limitations. Mantra repetition, *japa*, is the best antidote to the disease called fear — fear which turns you away from God, fear which destroys your principles. In fact, there is a proverb which says, "When danger approaches, sing to it." Remember, you are not your fear. As you chant the mantra, sustain the awareness "I am Consciousness, I am Bliss, I am the Self." Then you will fear nothing.

Shirdi Sai Baba's message has always been "Have no fear, I am with you." So, to develop this state of fearlessness, begin by trusting the words of the saints. They are with you. It is the absolute truth. There is another saying which goes: "Don't be afraid of tomorrow. God is already there."

With great respect, with great love, once again, I welcome you all with all my heart.

June 26, 1993

CHAPTER TWO

PURITY OF BEING

Sattva-saṃśhuddhi

WITH GREAT RESPECT AND GREAT LOVE, I welcome you all with all my heart.

One of the most fruitful ways of drawing grace into one's life is a heartfelt prayer. Prayers have great power. Of course, some people pray for negative things. Others pray for small advantages. To understand what to pray for, to seek the most beneficial blessings, you really have to contemplate carefully. A true prayer is a blessing in itself.

In an ancient Upanishadic hymn, a sage prays:

O Lord,
May my body become pure.
May I be free from impurity.
May I know myself as divine light.

O Lord,
May my mind become pure.
May my self become pure.
May I know myself as divine light.

O Lord,
May I realize You with my purified understanding.

May I realize the highest bliss with my purified understanding.
May I realize You who are the highest bliss
with my purified understanding.

Such simple words, and yet filled with power. The prayers of the sages reveal the Self because they have poured their own divine heart into their words. When we repeat the prayers they uttered, it purifies our hearts. There are other prayers, however, that arise spontaneously, without any contemplation at all; and they are no less pure or true.

The magnificent virtues are our theme. To explore them, we are taking the support of chapter sixteen of the *Bhagavad Gītā*, "The Song of the Lord." In this chapter, "The Yoga of the Division Between the Divine and the Demoniacal," Lord Krishna enumerates for Arjuna the virtues that help a person transcend the obstacles of life so that he or she may experience the Supreme Reality, the divinity that dwells in his or her own heart.

Virtues. You mustn't let the word scare you. "Oh, this or that is such a high ideal, how can *I* ever attain it?" Whatever you think, so you become. Therefore, you must watch your thoughts and cultivate the highest understanding of your own nature, lest your own mental processes pull you down. It is much better to aspire to these virtues than to fear them, better to experience even a tiny portion of any one of them than to wallow in misery.

Last night, we began with the virtue of fearlessness. It takes fearlessness to unveil the beauty of the great Self. Understand, we are not talking about ordinary fear, the kind that the body and mind naturally experience when their well-being is in jeopardy; we are talking about the deadly fear which separates a seeker from the knowledge of God. One of the basic teachings of Siddha Yoga is "See God in each other." Many people find it very difficult to put this into practice. Why? They are afraid. Afraid of what? Of the vision of God. Fear is the enemy that must be conquered before the teachings can come to life.

A Western mystic, Angelus Silesius, once said, "The Most High is absolutely without measure, as we know, and yet a human heart can enclose Him entirely!"

With the same sense of wonder, one of the scriptures of Kashmir Shaivism exclaims, "O Lord, You have hidden Yourself in the body of a human being. What a mystery!"

Within this human body lives the great Truth. It is all yours. Discover it.

The virtue that we're going to discuss tonight is purity of being, *sattva-samshuddhi.* The literal meaning of the word is very profound. *Sat* stands for the truth which is the essence of your being, inside and out; *shuddhi,* for purity. So, the absolute purity of the essence of your being is *sattva-samshuddhi.*

Now, when a person is born, it is true, he carries a heavy bundle of past impressions and consequences. He brings into this new life everything he has seen and felt and the fruits of all that he has done in the past. Why? Because whatever the senses do, the impressions of those actions lodge inside us.

You may think you are watching a harmless little movie, just to pass the time. But, you must understand, every bit of the action of that movie lodges in your system. You think you're going to have a very easy, quick little meal—just pizza. Understand, every ounce of oil in that pizza clings to the organs of your body, and this, in turn, affects the *nādīs,* the channels that run through the subtle body like veins. It takes a long, long time to purify them, and it is really not a joke at all. How many times have you bumped into an old friend, someone you haven't seen in several years, and been struck by the change in him? You think, "Oh my, has he aged! In five years!" But is it really the years? No. It is what he has eaten. It is what he has thought. It is what he's felt. It is what he's done. The impressions of his actions have stuck in his system.

Do you begin to see? On the one hand, you are carrying the impressions of past lifetimes; and on the other hand, you are performing actions now which have their own consequences and bear their own fruit. Therefore, the actions you do in the present moment are crucial. Either they continue to add momentum to the old actions, increasing their weight and their pull, or they change the direction and shift the balance. The result is either fortune or misfortune.

Purity of being, *sattva-samshuddhi,* evolves out of pure actions. No movie is "innocent." There is no such thing as a "simple" meal. Everything, even the news, affects you on a deep level. Haven't you often realized, hours after hearing a piece of news, that you are still saddened by it—or uplifted, as the case may be? News is news. Good or bad, it affects you. Whatever you feed to your ears stays inside you.

Very few human beings can process these things immediately. You have to be extremely disciplined to absorb or assimilate impressions from outside and process them so quickly that nothing remains in your system. If you try to bathe in a muddy pond, you are more likely to get dirty than clean. You may even drown in muck. In the same way, if you perform reckless impure actions, sooner or later you will be over your head in consequences.

The *Spanda Kārikās,* one of the fundamental scriptures of Kashmir Shaivism, says:

> *nijāśhuddhyāsamarthasya kartavyeṣhvabhilāṣhiṇaḥ /*
> *yadā kṣhobhaḥ pralīyeta tadā syāt paramaṃ padam //*

> An individual is incapacitated by his own impurity and is attached to actions. [1:9]

This is such a telling statement. Impurity eclipses the highest state and plunges you into false attachment at the same time. So, for example, when a person says that he is incapable of performing a pure action such as meditation, it raises a question. The vast Lord dwells in every heart. What stops a person from knowing this? The light of God burns brilliantly in every heart. As the poet-saint Kabir says, there is no such thing as a heart where there is no *sai,* no light. Then what stops a person from seeing it? What weakens a person so much that he does not have the power to go within?

The answer is, that person's own impurity—layers and layers of consequences, piles and piles of debris from the past. Not only is he staggering under the weight of his actions, he's attached to them.

These impurities are the result of three constant, deep-seated feelings: "I am imperfect; I am different; I am the doer, the author, of my own actions." Nothing is more destructive than these feelings, which Kashmir Shaivism calls the three *malas.* Because of them, a person goes round and round on the wheel of birth and death, trapped in his own limitations. He performs one degraded action after another. He becomes more and more enmeshed in his delusions. His vision is totally distorted.

It's a vicious circle. A person performs one misdeed and thinks, "What does it matter? I was bad to begin with." You drink one glass of alcohol and you say, "I might as well have two... Well, since I've had two, what's the harm in three?... After three, what does the fourth glass matter? I mean, I'm already drunk." In this way, within a few months, you are drinking four hundred glasses and you don't even realize it.

Finally, someone says, "Are you an alcoholic?"

And you say, "No. I have a sip here and there, but I can stop any time I want."

It is the same with every action you perform. Sometimes, a person starts talking to pass the time for an hour or two a day... at mealtimes. Pretty soon, it's taking three or four hours, just to catch up. The time comes when that person is talking in his sleep.

Then somebody says, "Don't you think you talk a little too much?"

And the person is flabbergasted. "Who, me? I hardly talk at all. Honestly! All I ever do is listen."

One action leads to another, and another, and another. A human being does not stop to think, and *that* is the biggest problem. Not impurities. Not the *malas.* But simply forgetting to ask the basic questions: "What am I doing? Where am I going? What do I really want?"

This morning I was talking to someone who is looking for another job—a better job, as she puts it, than the one she has—and she said, "You know, Gurumayi, I'm fighting for survival."

"What jungle do you live in?" I asked. "As far as I know, we are in North America. You have a wide range. You can do anything you want. It's not a matter of survival. It's a matter of choice." When you don't stop to think what you're saying, you allow every thought that goes through your head to control you.

A person who is deluded in this way sees the entire world through the filter of his own distortions. From the standpoint of the knowers of the Truth, this universe is a play of Consciousness. But for a person like this, the universe is a place of punishment. Everywhere he looks, he sees eyes filled with hatred. He finds a million faults with every place he goes. Everybody grates on him. The whole world is abrasive; and whatever happens, his discomfort only grows. If he's on the ground, he's afraid rats will take a piece out of him. If he's in the sky, he worries about flying dragons.

No place is sacred for him; no time is important, no person is good enough, and no relationship is sufficient. Nothing works. His impurities are so thick he can barely conceive of love, let alone ecstasy. Like a dog chasing its tail, he dizzies himself into thinking there is nothing more to life. He is it.

When a meditator says he or she is suffering, it makes you wonder. "Does this person contemplate? Does he read Baba's books? Does she ever perform one kind action for another person?" Truly, if you perform a single act of kindness for another human being, your suffering is erased, and this is the truth. Consequently, when you see someone like this coming again and again to tell you his woes, you realize that no matter what you say, nothing enters him. He or she lives behind a glass wall of miseries; he can see the light, but he will not let it in. You wonder, "Doesn't he ever try to turn within? Or is the attachment to every action and emotion so intense that he never thinks of controlling himself, no matter how much he suffers?" If that is true, he will only become increasingly fragmented, and more powerless, and never experience the great Truth that abides within him, whole and full of bliss.

When it comes to purity, most people are like Sheikh Nasruddin. Once the watchman of a small village found his old friend Nasruddin wandering through the streets at midnight. "What are you doing out so late?" he said. "I lost a lot of sleep," Nasruddin replied. "And I'm trying to find it." That is exactly the way people look for purity—on the outside. They want somebody else to make them pure. They want somebody else to inspire *shuddha bhāvana,* pure feelings, pure thoughts, and motivate them to perform good actions.

When things go wrong, what do you do? Do you look at yourself? Or do you always want to blame God, the Guru, and the world? Does it ever occur to you that by assuming responsibility you can make a great change in your life? Or are you like a lazy tiger who just sits around all day waiting for somebody else to bring it food?

What do you do? Do you keep yourself in check? Or do you allow your thoughts to run at random? Do you let your mind enter any room it wants without your permission? Do you hold the reins, so that when your mind does run wild, you can bring it back? Or do you just wait for the Almighty to do all the work? Which is it? What is your way of looking at the world and yourself? Have you ever thought about it? If you haven't, think about it now.

Everyone says so many mishaps take place; so many accidents, so many terrible things happen all the time. It is wonderful, isn't it, to sit around a coffee table and talk about who is bombing whom, who is stealing whose money, who is taking whom to court. But do you ever stop to think you are also responsible for what happens in this world? In your own home? In your own backyard? How do you maintain yourself?

Think about it. Are you like Nasruddin going out to catch up on his sleep? Or are you your own greater Self who knows where to look, where to be, what to feel? What are your emotions like? Do your feelings have a life of their own? Do they pop up whenever they want to? Are they subversive? Do they cut you down? Or do they come from a deeper source, one that is in tune with time and place, and the needs of other people?

What is the remedy? The sages say, Wake up! Cultivate this divine virtue: purity of being, *sattva-samshuddhi.* This is a very rich subject. As an attainment, as a state, *sattva-samshuddhi* means much more than just cleansing the mind, strengthening the intellect, purifying the body and the heart. *Sattva-samshuddhi* means becoming completely established in purity.

How can you purify your being? You begin with the simple things. First, purify your actions. When a thought arises, pause for a second before you act on it. If it is not a nourishing thought, let it dissolve back into Consciousness. Secondly, sever your false attachment to impure actions. If a friend makes a comment about your behavior that goes against the grain, don't reject it out of hand. Listen for the voice of God in it. Even if you don't want to accept that particular piece of advice, or criticism, or instruction, don't shove it aside. Contemplate it. God speaks through many mouths. Finally, develop a healthy discipline. There is no other way to take control of your senses, your habits, your emotions, and your thoughts.

"If a man sets his heart on benevolence," said Confucius, "he will be free from evil." In this, your resolution counts a great deal. When you set your heart on something that is completely uplifting, you gradually become free from impurities. Wherever you place your heart, that is where you end up. It is very difficult for someone who is not able to stick to a steady and clean resolve to work his way out of delusion.

However, if you truly believe in grace, if you have faith in the benevolent hand of God, if you really give your life to the highest Truth, then you do not have to work at attaining purity of being. All you have to do is allow yourself to be purified in the fire of yoga, in the fire of God's love. In time, every action you perform will be golden. Every thought will be thorough and constructive. Your whole being will become radiant with the light of wisdom.

One of the greatest scriptures on the mind is called the *Yoga Vāsishtha*. In it the sage Vasishtha says:

yad-idaṃ bhāsate kiñchit-tat-tasyaiva nirāmayam /
kachanaṃ kāchakasyaiva kāntasyā 'timaṇeriva //

Whatever shines is the pure light of that Supreme Being.
His light surrounds us like a transcendental jewel. [3.21:68]

That light exists in the heart. The moment you experience your own purity, you become transparent, and the light shines through. This light actually has a taste. It is nectar.

Baba Muktananda gave us beautiful guidelines for staying in the ashram, to develop and maintain purity of being. In a satsang in Ganeshpuri, he once said, "One does not improve just by being physically present in the ashram. One improves by fully accepting the ashram discipline." In other words, you must do more than accept the discipline of the ashram. You must make it your own. As long as you think of it as belonging to somebody else, you will not experience any joy in it and you won't be able to grow.

In fact, sometimes when Baba talked about living in the ashram, he used to say, "Rats and cats and dogs also live in the ashram. Why not? Crows and cockroaches and pigeons live here, too. If you live in the ashram the way they do, you are not going to discover anything at all."

Baba went on to say, "If you were to take a fatal dose of poison in a hospital, nobody could save you, even there. You can only be cured of a malady if you stick to the doctor's prescription. Likewise, while living in the ashram, you can be saved from the ocean of *samsāra*, the cycle of birth and death, only if you are devoted to the great Self, the *ātman*. If you are devoted to pleasure and mundane things, even here, you will sink. Any ashramite can become slightly lazy and careless in the beginning, but if he is not checked, his bad habits will only increase. Hence the discipline. If your heart does not change, you may spend any length of time in the ashram, but there is no guarantee that you will not fall." Something to remember.

People used to ask Baba, "Babaji, so many people have been near you for so many years. Why do some of them seem to have made no progress at all?"

Baba would say, "There is nothing I can do. It is all up to them. Whoever wants to make progress, can. He doesn't have to be near me. All he has to do is follow the teachings, perform the practices, and remember the Guru. In no time at all, he makes great progress."

It is what you hold in your mind that inspires progress on the spiritual path. *Sattva-samshuddhi*, purity of being, is a level of awareness. It takes place depending on what you are thinking and feeling, and especially, on your actions.

All sorts of people come to stay in the ashram. There are some who are able to absorb the teachings intellectually. They understand the teachings very well, and they are also able to give the teachings to others. The ancient philosophy of Vedanta has an expression for people like this. It says such a person is like the ladle that serves the dessert.

Baba used to tell this anecdote with such relish. He would say, "You know the long ladle that you dip into a big vessel of *kheer*, the sweet pudding everyone loves so much?... Well, as it is serving the *kheer*, the ladle keeps saying, 'Mmmm... this is *yummy*! Have a little more, have a little more. It's so delicious, have some more...' And it keeps serving, and serving, until somebody asks, 'Have *you* tasted it?' "

Then the ladle answers, "There's plenty here, I have so much in this vessel. Please have some more. Let me serve you."

But the person persists. He keeps asking, "Haven't you ever tasted it for yourself?" until finally the ladle hesitates a moment, and says, "I'm not sure I know what you mean. I'll have to think about it."

So many people understand the teachings intellectually. They know *A* comes before *B* and so on. They know the whole alphabet by heart. But their lifestyle does not match the teachings at all, and when you ask them the meaning of what they are saying, of what they are giving others, they don't know.

To develop *sattva-samshuddhi*, the purity of your actions is the pivotal element. Your actions shape your character. They reflect your inner universe. They can be a burning torch that lights the way to paradise, or they can be so base that they bring doom to you and your world. Simply to be comfortable with yourself, even to attain that little bit, your conscience has to be clear. Otherwise, you're restless and ill at ease. Using that as a measure, you can imagine how much purity is necessary in order to perceive the light of the inner Self, or how much purity you must have to attain liberation.

Have you ever come up in darshan, and sat yourself down, blocking everyone else, and asked, "Can you give me liberation now?"

And then, a hall monitor says, "Can you please move over?"

You say indignantly, "I am asking Gurumayi a question!" And you stay right where you are. After a while, Gurumayi turns toward you again, and you repeat your question, making yourself look sweet again. "Can you give me liberation right now?"

Gurumayi listens and looks away again. The hall monitor says, "Can you please move over? You're blocking the line."

And this time it makes you furious. You turn to the hall monitor and you snap, "I'm asking a question! It's very important!"

You want liberation but you cannot perform the simplest action of getting out of the way.

The philosopher of the *Tao Te Ching* says: "Simple in actions and in thoughts, you return to the source of being." That is exactly the way to attain purity of being, by becoming simpler and simpler. Purity of being is a magnificent virtue to cultivate.

Once again, in this, as in any virtue, discipline is paramount. Really, it is discipline in thoughts, feelings, and in actions that produces harmony and well-being. When you keep yourself in check and eliminate all the dregs of past actions through spiritual practices, then the vision of the heart stands before you.

Last night, in our discussion of fearlessness, it was said that one of the best means of overcoming fear is to repeat the mantra. It is also one of the best ways of experiencing this virtue. Truly, the mantra is the best remedy. It is a very subtle tonic, as Baba once said. Just as the vibration of a sound echoes in an empty space, so the sound of the mantra fills the empty space of your entire being with its own perfect purity.

As you get up and leave the hall tonight and move about, watch your step and watch your mind. An agitated mind leads you to your own destruction. A mind that is in touch with its true Self, with its essence, leads to lightness wherever you go. So as you leave the hall, make an effort to stay simple in thought and simple in actions. Also, pay attention to the state of your heart. Notice how the movement or the silence of the heart affects your entire being. Watch what you eat. Watch what you say.

When you go to bed tonight, remember to repeat the mantra. It is always beneficial to read something from the scriptures before you go to sleep, to purify your thoughts during the night. The simplest thing to do is repeat the mantra until you fall asleep. It is the best and easiest way to experience the purity of your being. Baba always said, basically, everyone is good.

With great respect, with great love, I welcome you all with all my heart.

June 27, 1993

CHAPTER THREE

STEADFASTNESS IN YOGA

Yoga-vyavasthiti

WITH GREAT RESPECT, WITH GREAT LOVE, I welcome you all with all my heart.

This entire universe has come from nothingness. Yet it consists of myriad subjects, objects, names, and forms. People get very caught up in all these appearances. They lose themselves in the forest of what is and what is not. No one escapes this entirely. It is part of our nature. But the same questions about reality lead people in different directions — some to the utmost delusion and others to liberation. The path that stretches between these two points is called yoga.

The mind needs something to hold on to. On its own it flounders. Without support or direction, the mind goes in circles. It drifts with every wind like a ship with no rudder and no hand on the wheel. Yoga steadies the mind so that it falls, as a matter of course, into alignment with the deepest rhythms of its own nature.

The *Avadhūta Stotram* is a beautiful hymn in praise of the great renunciant Bhagawan Nityananda. One of its verses describes him like this:

yoga-pūrṇaṃ tapo-mūrtiṃ prema-pūrṇaṃ sudarśhanam /
jñāna-pūrṇaṃ kṛipā-mūrtiṃ nityānandaṃ namāmyaham //

> Perfect in yoga, an embodiment of austerity, full of love, of auspicious countenance, perfect in knowledge, an embodiment of grace — to that Nityananda, I bow. [16]

Let this thought support you. Allow this awareness to direct you. Like Bhagawan Nityananda, you can actually become filled with the power of yoga, filled with the power of knowledge.

Even to hold this idea in your mind is liberating. You have to have a greater goal. You need a higher aspiration. This is something every seeker must understand. To save his soul, he must stop sitting on a haystack. Otherwise, he will burst into flame at the drop of a match. He must stop wading in muddy ponds. Otherwise, he will never know purity. He must stop concentrating on other people's faults and weaknesses. Otherwise he will destroy the well-being of his own mind. A true seeker must refuse to run other people down or eye their possessions, whatever they may be — good qualities or bad qualities, good conduct or bad, poverty or wealth. A true seeker, in fact, turns his attention away from other people's behavior and examines his own heart.

We have been looking at the magnificent virtues, one by one, very carefully, so that we may translate them into action. Once again, these virtues already exist within us. All we have to do is uncover them.

The first one that we looked at was fearlessness. Remember? We came to see how formidable an enemy fear is. To attain anything in our lives, we must overcome fear. We must find our way to fearlessness, which removes all diseases and lets a seeker merge into God.

Purity of being is the second virtue mentioned in chapter sixteen of the *Bhagavad Gītā*, and this we also explored: constantly performing self-inquiry to make sure no rust collects around our hearts; keeping ourselves in check; being as clear as crystal; not letting even a trace of dishonor diminish the purity of our inner state.

Now we come to *yoga-vyavasthiti*, steadfastness in yoga. Let us begin by asking ourselves a very important question: What is yoga?

In the *Bhagavad Gītā*, Lord Krishna gives three clear and very beautiful definitions of the word, so we don't have to search high and low for the meaning, nor do we need to sit here and scratch our heads, thinking feverishly, "What is it? What can it be? What is yoga?" Lord Krishna was very compassionate. The first definition he gave Arjuna is:

> *yogasthaḥ kuru karmāṇi saṅgaṃ tyaktvā dhanaṇjaya /*
> *siddhyasiddhyoḥ samo bhūtvā samatvaṃ yoga uchyate //*
>
> Steadfast in yoga, perform all your actions,
> having abandoned attachment,
> and become indifferent to success and failure.
> It is said that evenness of mind is yoga. [2:48]

Another definition is:

> *buddhiyukto jahātīha ubhe sukṛitaduṣhkṛite /*
> *tasmād yogāya yujyasva yogaḥ karmasu kauśhalam //*
>
> One whose wisdom is established
> casts off, in this world, both good and evil actions.
> Therefore, devote yourself to yoga!
> Yoga is skill in action. [2:50]

A third definition of yoga that Lord Krishna gave Arjuna is:

> *taṃ vidyād duḥkhasaṃyoga-viyogaṃ yogasaṃjñitam /*
> *sa niśhchayena yoktavyo yogo' nirviṇṇachetasā //*
>
> Let this, the severance of union with pain,
> be known as yoga;
> Yoga must be practiced with determination
> and with an undismayed mind. [6:23]

These are the three principal definitions of yoga in the *Bhagavad Gītā*. Evenness of mind is yoga, *samatvaṃ yoga uchyate*. Yoga is skill in action, *yogaḥ karmasu kauśhalam*. Severing the union with pain is yoga, *duḥkhasaṃyoga-viyogam*.

Just pronouncing the word *yoga* automatically stimulates *rasa* inside you. *Rasa* is the nectar, the flavor, the fountain of life. To be steadfast in yoga is to acknowledge your reverence for the goal of spiritual life. It means you know how important it is to hold on to the golden cup of yoga. It means you embrace the path with great care and gratitude; and that fact alone, the simple conscious recognition that you cherish yoga, is enough to fill you with the great yogic feelings: moderation, discipline, regularity.

The other morning, after we chanted the *Guru Gītā*, a woman came up in the darshan line and said, "Gurumayi, my mind is so restless. It wanders and wanders, even during the *Guru Gītā*. I cannot make it be quiet. Can you please do something?" Her eyes were moist. Her lips were quivering. Her whole body was positively begging for help. Nevertheless, although she was describing the restlessness of her mind and the way it was driving her crazy, the most noticeable thing about her was the strength of her intention. She was so focused. There was such steadfastness in her description of her wavering mind.

So you cannot say she lacked evenness of mind. Not really. Her explanation had too much power. So did the way she allowed the experience of restlessness to continue. It was powerful, yes. But you couldn't call it yoga. She was completely caught up in success and failure, chanting well or chanting badly. She was thoroughly absorbed in her attachment to the fluctuations of her mind; and that was her focus — not the *Guru Gītā*. This woman has a great ability to zero in; only she was zeroing in on the wrong thing. She knew very well what her mind was doing, but she was only steadfast in her delusions, not in the purity of yoga.

People who are cynical demonstrate the same great steadfastness. They say, "This can't work! I don't care what anybody says, I don't believe it. Once upon a time I loved God. But not now! All this is just a fad! I can't accept it! I won't!" Such steadfastness in cynicism!

Lord Krishna advised Arjuna to be steadfast in yoga. What did he mean? We can think about this in different ways. For example, he must have been saying, "Don't follow in the footsteps of a turbulent mind. Don't pursue the desires of the impure mind. Don't retrace the patterns of past impressions. Don't dwell on infatuations left over from the past. Don't loiter in the dark corners of your mind."

Samatvaṃ yoga uchyate, evenness of mind is yoga. When you abandon your attachment to negative actions, when you renounce relationships that can only bring about your downfall, then you are becoming established in yoga. You are not sinking in the quicksand of illusions. You are in the process of building a very solid foundation. The entire landscape of the mind spreads out before you, and you learn to watch it without being perturbed. You witness the past, the present, and the future, but you don't allow any of it to affect your inner stability.

This is evenness of mind. This is yoga.

Steadfastness, or perseverance, as it is sometimes called, is very highly valued in all walks of life. There can be no true happiness or joy without it, and no lasting attainment. In Sanskrit, the word for perseverance has several distinct definitions. One of them is *dīrgha prayatna*, which means prolonged endeavor. Another one is *sthairya*, which has four very different meanings: firmness, patience, consistency, and steadfastness.

When you come across variations in the meaning of a word, it gives you an indication of how profound that word is. You cannot simply take it at face value; you have to go deeper. It is like gazing at the ocean from the shore. Of course, it looks vast, magnificent, and awesome. But how much vaster, how much more magnificent and awesome it is when you dive deep into its depths. You become a part of the ocean then. In the same way, perseverance and steadfastness in yoga turn you into the Truth. Then you are no longer watching the Truth from a distance, like a spectator. You are living in the Truth. You think of the Truth, and all your actions are true. You don't have to go looking for honesty. Whatever you do is filled with Truth.

Someone once asked Baba Muktananda, "How is it possible to forget a clear realization or lose an attainment?" This is a great fear, isn't it? You always want to know, "Will I lose it?" So many people ask, "Once my Kundalini Shakti is awakened at the base of the spine through the Guru's grace, will it ever become dormant again?" Or people ask, "Once I see the Truth, will I forget it again?"

Baba answered, "You can make a realization permanent only through persevering, steadfast practice. It is a strange irony that there are certain seekers who, after attaining the inner awakening of the Shakti by the Guru, begin to neglect the ashram, the Guru, and their sadhana, the spiritual practices. And the result is that the Shakti, the great energy, begins to neglect them, too."

What a concept! What a warning! The other day, a couple of girls went up to two other girls their own age, who are very new to Siddha Yoga, and said, "We see Gurumayi is paying a lot of attention to you. We just wanted to tell you, it won't last. This is a particular phase of sadhana; it's called the honeymoon. Believe me, any day now, Gurumayi's going to start ignoring you, so you'd better be careful."

These two newcomers got very frightened and upset. So they went to one of the old-timers, someone who's been living in the ashram for a good many years, and asked her for advice. They said, "The prospect of losing Gurumayi's attention frightens us. We don't want to lose Gurumayi's pleasure. What can we do? What can we do?"

And this person, who is steadfast in yoga and in the dharma of ashram life, said, "Don't be afraid. Right now, you are paying so much attention to Gurumayi and to the ashram. You come to the *Guru Gītā* every day. You are interested in meditation. You're enthusiastic about all the practices. You are both drenched in the love of the Guru and the experience of the Shakti. What is there to be afraid of? Start worrying about losing the Guru's attention when you start wasting time and hanging out with the boys in the ashram, when you start thinking, 'Ah, ashram life is s-o-o-o-o boring...' You run the risk of losing the Guru's attention then. But until then, don't worry, don't be frightened; just continue your practices."

And that is a fact. There is no honeymoon phase in sadhana. It is a prolonged endeavor from beginning to end. You don't receive the Guru's attention one day and lose it the next. Grace is abundant. As Baba always said, it all depends on how much you expose your heart to grace, how much you hide your heart from grace. As long as your heart is completely open to the Guru, and to all those who carry the flame of God in their hearts, as long as you are saturated with the longing to experience the Truth, you have absolutely nothing to fear.

Baba continued, "Sometimes after a little bit of realization or a few experiences, a person begins to think that he has become perfect. But he forgets that one has to work diligently for a long time to stabilize what he has attained. Therefore, continue to practice steadfastly for a prolonged period and your attainment will also become permanent."

As interested as you may be in exploring all the different avenues of life, you also need to be steadfast in your spiritual search. So this is a very necessary virtue, call it what you will: perseverance, steadfastness, firmness, or singleness of purpose. You cannot get along without it.

The second definition Lord Krishna gave to Arjuna is *yogaḥ karmasu kauśhalam*, yoga is skill in action. In this verse, Arjuna was asked to devote himself to yoga without falling prey to good and evil deeds.

Most people act with great fierceness to show how right they are and how wrong others are. They want to prove how good their intentions are and how destructive or self-serving everybody else is. So there is no purity in their action. It is tainted by a holier-than-thou attitude. Have you ever performed an action like this? Whether the action itself is right or wrong, good or evil, generally speaking, people strive most of all to get the upper hand. Does this ring a bell? People who behave like this — and most do — are living by the law of the jungle. Survival of the fittest. Whoever speaks the loudest wins. And therefore, though many of their actions may turn out well at times, you cannot say that they are established in yoga.

Yoga is skill in action, remember? What exactly is this skill? It is the wisdom to separate your lower self from your higher Self. It is the skill to distinguish your own motivation, to be able to tell whether you are performing an action for your own glorification or for the benefit of the world you live in. It is the power to struggle with your own darkness and keep your eyes on the light. It is the ability to keep temptations at bay and act with integrity.

Of course, all sorts of obstacles are bound to arise. It's practically a law of nature—the moment you decide you are going to get up early every morning and meditate, a million emergencies come up. If you are not steadfast in yoga, then you never develop the knack, the subtle ability, of warding them off and fulfilling your highest dharma, no matter what. It takes tremendous stamina to perform spiritual practices. Things don't always go the way you plan. Actually, they almost never do. So you must be vigilant. You cannot rely on your good karma or the merits you have inherited from your ancestors. You must learn to rely on your Self alone. That is why you practice yoga.

A wonderful writer once said, "If your ship doesn't come in, swim out to it." Now that is yoga in action. It is not what most people do. They toss out two cents' worth of advice and expect millions of favors in return. They perform one kind action and wonder why the universe isn't grateful. Isn't it amazing what people do and what they expect in return, what people *don't* do and what they expect in return? No one wants to put in a sustained effort to make his or her life a paradise, but everybody wants other people to put themselves out. "Why didn't you come? I waited so long. Why didn't you phone me? Why didn't you write to me on my birthday? Why? Why didn't you do this? Why didn't you do that? Why don't you say something sweet to me? Why don't you? Why don't you ever sing me a song?"

It's always somebody else who should be doing all these wonderful things. Some other people commonly referred to as "they." Actually, while they're at it, "they" ought to develop all these great virtues, too. After all, you tell yourself, "they" are the ones who need them, isn't that so?

This summer, we offered a course called "How to Face Death." During those five days, a lot of people woke up to the fact of their own mortality. One person remarked, "This entire life is just a preparation for the moment you draw your last breath, isn't it?" Now that understanding is incredibly valuable. The last moments of life, the passage into oblivion, must happen efficiently and gracefully. You must meet the transition armed with all your good merits.

On some level, everyone knows this. How much effort a person is willing to make is another story. A lot of people get very excited about liberation, God, the Truth, serving humanity, making this world a better paradise, developing virtues, experiencing the Guru's love, becoming strong in mind and heart, ending hunger, and so on. Yet, how many people really commit themselves to these great causes, revelations, insights, actions, and aspirations? That is a big question. If it remains a question too long, you are in deep trouble, you are in hot water.

Why? Look at a question mark. It even looks like a hook, especially in the Spanish language where it's written upside down. If you don't get yourself off the hook, your ignorance will stifle you. That is a miserable life, indeed — not only fading into oblivion but also living in oblivion. A French writer once said, "One should want only one thing and want it constantly. Then one is sure of getting it. But I desire everything equally. Consequently, I end up with nothing. Each time I discover, and always too late, that one thing had come while I was running after another."

In his spiritual autobiography, *Play of Consciousness*, Baba Muktananda wrote, "If a rich man doesn't guard his wealth or a good man his virtue, these things are soon lost. In the same way, a seeker who lives without discipline and regularity weakens his Shakti."

The Guru doesn't take his attention away from you. You allow yourself to lose it by letting the Shakti inside you grow weaker. Whether the result of this negligence is a doubt or a negativity, they are not what really matters. Once you have been awakened to the truth of your own being, you must learn to nurture that experience in every way possible.

Now, for the third definition of yoga. Lord Krishna says to Arjuna, "Let this, the severance of union with pain, be known as yoga." Then he adds, "Yoga must be practiced with determination and with an undismayed mind."

Duḥkhasaṃyoga-viyogam, severing the union with pain: this is such an elevated definition of yoga. What a relief it is to know you can actually divorce yourself from pain. It is no exaggeration to say the whole world suffers. People suffer; so do trees, oceans, birds, and animals. The earth itself suffers. Even the heavens suffer — from all the rockets and satellites, the invasion of pollutants, and revolving space stations. Everything suffers. Suffering may have different causes and vary in length or intensity, but fundamentally it is all the same. Some people suffer because of lack of money. Some suffer because of lack of love. Some suffer from low self-esteem. Others suffer because of violence. But ultimately, everyone suffers because of ignorance.

The Indian scriptures speak about three types of afflictions. The first is called *ādhyātmika,* which is suffering caused by the body or mind. This kind of suffering is generated internally by ailments in the body or unsatisfied desires of the mind. Baba always said that this type of suffering is primarily caused by undisciplined living and irregularity of every kind.

The second kind of affliction is called *ādhibhautika,* which is suffering caused by nature, through the world and the creatures around us. Sometimes it comes in the form of a flood or a drought or an earthquake, or a region is invaded by swarms of insects. In some places, or in certain seasons, it may be either too cold or too hot to sustain life easily.

The third affliction is called *ādhidaivika.* This is the suffering caused by the gods, by celestial beings, and by spirits. According to the ancient scriptures, every single thing in this universe has its own deity; and when these powers, these deities, are not happy with you, they create problems. Whenever we chant mantras to open a program, we end by singing *Om shāntih shāntih shāntih.* We repeat the word *shāntih,* peace, three times, as a prayer that we may be protected from these three kinds of calamity.

All suffering involves pain. As long as a seeker fails to understand that he can heal his own wounds, that he has the power to put an end to his anguish, he remains married to pain. So, Lord Krishna explains to Arjuna, yoga is severing the union with pain. Think about this for a moment. Isn't it true, you flirt with pain? Don't you court pain? Go to sleep with pain and wake up with pain, all in the name of experiencing pleasure? Is there anything you do which doesn't eventually end in one form of pain or another?

There is a beautiful song by the poet-saint Purandardas. Every time I hear it, it brings tears to my eyes. At one point it says, "In the beginning it seems so pleasurable. But unfailingly it turns into pain in the end."

Sense pleasures are so gratifying in the beginning, but there has never been a time in anyone's life when they have not spoiled and turned into pain. Yoga severs the union with pain. So there is relief. There is freedom. When you become steadfast in yoga, you can cut away pain at its roots. Still, some people like being married to pain. They are very faithful spouses. Pain is their deity. Pain is their glory. Misfortune means everything to them.

Pain remains as it is or gets worse, as it can, all because you are constantly trying to suppress it or duck it one way or another. Sometimes you even refuse to admit your suffering to yourself. But the more you ignore pain, the greater it becomes. Sooner or later, you have to undergo the pain you have ignored. Does that surprise you? Do you think the Guru will wave a magic wand and that will be the end of pain? Why don't you think about changing your relationship to pain instead?

Once someone asked Baba this question: "You said that in order to be able to accept suffering with gratitude, it is necessary to learn a new language. Would you please tell us how?" Baba answered, "This new language emerges when you suffer again and again in your life. To accept suffering as something good, to bear it with courage and steadfastness, that is the new language. To realize that one's suffering is well deserved, to accept it cheerfully, and endure it with fortitude, that is what I meant by learning a new language."

In other words, Baba is asking a seeker to accept his pain instead of trying to avoid it. He calls steadfastness a new language.

By that he means you must learn to see pain from a new perspective. This doesn't mean you put yourself down, saying, "I am a sinner, I deserve to suffer." Not at all. You understand that you must undergo this pain to wash away the impurities you have accumulated. It is necessary so that the light of your own Self can blaze once again.

Baba says, accept this pain cheerfully. In order to do that, you have to tap into the source of bliss that lies within you. You have to do yoga. Baba is asking the seeker to be a warrior. In his eyes, you are not a victim. Not if you have the strength and faith to accept this pain and bring it to an end.

The German author Goethe said, "Only he earns his freedom and existence who daily wins them anew." Every day perform yoga with fresh inspiration. Attaining freedom doesn't mean it's all over and you will never have anything to worry about again. Freedom must be nourished. You have to make the experience of freedom new every single day. Your life is yours, of course. Still, you have to own it over and over again. You have to renew this contract every day. Otherwise, it becomes old; and who knows? There may be a loophole. So you have to keep renewing your contract with life.

Therefore, in this verse Lord Krishna tells Arjuna, "This yoga should be practiced with determination and with an undismayed mind." This is such valuable advice. Practice this yoga of divorcing pain with an undesponding mind. His first point, determination, is something that everyone understands. Sometimes, you just have to go for it. As the *Yoga Vāsishtha* says, put forth the effort, grind your teeth, and don't waver. But the second point, to proceed with an undismayed mind, is extremely difficult to practice. It is so easy to get upset. And yet Lord Krishna asks you to face your pain without dismay. In the process of getting rid of your troubles, don't get rid of your Self, the great Self. In the name of overcoming difficulties, don't overthrow your Self. In the name of rescuing a drowning person, don't let your Self go under. In the name of freeing yourself from pain, don't bind your Self. Let your mind be undesponding, undismayed.

You really need a clear mind to understand the cause of pain and liberate yourself from it. The poet-saint Jnaneshwar Maharaj said, if you make a resolution that is beneficial, stick to it. Don't depart from it. Don't be like Mark Twain, who once said, "To cease smoking is the easiest thing I ever did; I ought to know, because I have done it a thousand times." Be steadfast in the vows you make. Be determined. Practice this without faltering and you will find your way to freedom.

To become steadfast in yoga is to become established in the highest Truth. In the fire of yoga, the dregs of the mind, the unsteadiness of the heart, the impurities in the body are all burned to ashes. With sustained effort and resolve, you do overcome the turbulence of the mind, the aimlessness of action, and the threefold afflictions. You regain a body of light. You experience your own true nature. God dwells within you as you. It becomes a reality. Love becomes a reality. As Rumi said, "Keep His commands constantly in view. Then suddenly the bird of grace will fly down."

It has been a long day, filled with many contemplations and many negativities, filled with many resolutions and many new departures, with many teachings and many difficulties. Therefore, let us rejuvenate ourselves with our own good companion, and that is the *prāna,* the inbreath and the outbreath. Allow your perception to become clearer. Allow all your thoughts to settle down quietly. Allow the body to become silent. Allow your heart to become attentive to the sound of the breath. As you breathe in and breathe out slowly, become more and more steadfast in yoga.

With great respect and great love, I welcome you all with all my heart.

July 10, 1993

Virtues will support your god given light —
they provide stability + guidance when you go the wrong path. — they protect you

CHAPTER FOUR

STEADFASTNESS IN KNOWLEDGE

Jñāna-vyavasthiti

WITH GREAT RESPECT AND LOVE, I welcome you all with all my heart.

You have been given a tremendous assignment to cultivate the great virtues, the very ones that you have always been afraid of. Many people have mentioned how intimidating the prospect of developing these virtues is for them. Once these virtues are fully developed within you, they say, you have to live up to them. You mustn't allow this kind of fear to destroy your own inner goodness. Why should you fear your own great Self? This mighty power is the innermost part of your own nature. You have been born with it, you live every moment of your life with it, and finally you will merge back into it. It is much better to recognize your own Self than to flee from it, and along with this act of Self-recognition, to experience the magnificent virtues that you carry within you. If the responsibility is great, then rise to the challenge.

These virtues are like dharma; they will protect you whenever you take the wrong path. Without them, you have no inner security. So many people experience weakness, and they have no support. They don't believe in God entirely, they can't accept the

Guru's grace, and they are unable to let other people's support into their lives. Why? Because they have not cultivated their own inner virtues; they are not in touch with their own innate goodness or the mercy that is an inherent part of their own nature.

Tonight we will look at the virtue of steadfastness in knowledge. By knowledge, here, we mean knowledge of the Self, knowledge of the Truth. This is wisdom, far removed from the sort of worldly information that you gather by watching television or listening to the radio, by reading or by gossiping. The highest knowledge cannot be acquired this way. You cannot even grasp it by reading descriptions of it in books.

Every scripture holds the man of knowledge in high esteem. In Siddha Yoga, we worship knowledge. The Lord Himself praises one who holds knowledge within himself. In the *Bhagavad Gītā* Lord Krishna says:

> *chaturvidhā bhajante māṃ janāh sukṛitino 'rjuna /*
> *ārto jijñāsurarthārthī jñānī cha bharatarṣhabha //*
>
> Four kinds of virtuous people worship Me, O Arjuna:
> those who are in distress, those who seek wealth,
> those who seek knowledge,
> and those who are wise. [7:16]
>
> *teṣhām jñānī nityayukta eka bhaktir viśhiṣhyate /*
> *priyo hi jñānino 'tyartham ahaṃ sa cha mama priyaḥ //*
>
> Of them, the wise person, eternally steadfast,
> devoted to the Supreme alone, is the best.
> I am exceedingly dear to the one who is immersed in wisdom,
> and he is dear to Me. [7:17]
>
> *udārāḥ sarva evāite jñānī tvātmaiva me matam /*
> *āsthitaḥ sa hi yuktātmā mām evānuttamāṃ gatim //*
>
> All of these seekers are noble indeed,
> but the one immersed in wisdom

I consider to be My very Self.
He whose mind is steadfast abides in Me alone,
the supreme goal. [7:18]

Even in your daily life, haven't you noticed, when somebody gives you good advice or reveals deep understanding, a feeling of immense gratitude and respect wells up in you? No matter what you are going through, or how difficult life is, you want to embrace that piece of advice and you genuinely like that person. If this is the case with you, imagine how much the Lord must love one who holds true knowledge within himself and remains aware of it twenty-four hours a day.

The other night a person came up in darshan and said, "Gurumayi, I have come out of the dark tunnel. Now, I am feeling very, very good."

I thanked God mentally for taking care of this man who had been in turmoil for so long. And then in the next breath he said, "But I still haven't seen the Blue Pearl."

I looked at him and said, "Your difficulties have ended; that's something to be thankful for."

"But... but I haven't seen the Blue Pearl. After all these years!" Then he said, "I am going to take the Blue Pearl Course." He looked straight into my eyes, meaningfully, hinting that the Blue Pearl had better be there when he was.

No one is ever satisfied. No one is able to experience contentment. Why couldn't this man relish the joy of being free from difficulties instead of washing it away with a desire for a vision of the Blue Pearl? It is such a profound relief to know that there comes a time when, through your sadhana, through your prolonged effort, you can actually overcome the troubles of the mind, the difficulties of the body, or the circumstances of your life. *That is jñāna, that is knowledge* — learning to be content with whatever happens, with however much or little you receive. When you learn to relish each moment in your life, know that you have become steadfast in knowledge. That is when the Blue Pearl may reveal itself, not when you go chasing after it, not on demand.

When you become steadfast in the knowledge of the Self, what do you really know? What can you say about it? The Vedas are the most ancient scriptures of India. No one composed the Vedas. They are the eternal wisdom which was revealed to the sages in deep states of meditation. Each of the four Vedas has a *mahāvākya,* a great utterance, which sums up its essential teachings. These great statements are the fruit of the Vedas, the gifts of the sages, steadfast in knowledge.

The *Rig Veda* declares: *prajñānaṃ brahma,* "The Absolute is Consciousness."

The *Atharva Veda* declares: *ayam ātmā brahma,* "The Self is the Absolute."

The *Sāma Veda* declares: *tat tvam asi,* "Thou art That."

The *Yajur Veda* declares: *aham brahmāsmi,* "I am the Absolute."

Each of these statements expresses the essential identity of the individual soul with the Absolute. In fact, *aham brahmāsmi* is the awareness that Baba imparted to all his swamis, the people who became monks, who dedicated their lives to serving humanity with the understanding that God exists in everybody. "I am the Absolute." This refers to the pure "I," to perfect I-consciousness. It has nothing to do with the petty ego. It comes from the deepest inner experience.

The other day, someone said she was doing *tādāsana,* the hatha yoga posture known as the mountain pose, and she finally had the experience of gliding into meditation. Over the years, she had heard the process of meditation described in this way many times. Still, she always thought *she* had to do it. She had applied herself to the attempt, with great effort and fastidiousness. The other night, however, standing in the mountain pose, she made no effort. As her body went into perfect balance, her mind became quiet and she slipped into meditation. She found herself in a deep state which she had never known before. It was so blissful, filled with a delight so pure she could not think of an analogy for it. It was indescribable.

Aham brahmāsmi, "I am the Absolute." It comes. It springs forth in this place of stillness. When you try simply to repeat the words, they may not make much sense to you. But when that state arises inside you, either in meditation or by the grace of the Guru, the experience is unmistakable. Baba imparted this wisdom. He planted the seed. So, believe in the Guru's grace and allow the experience of the Absolute to emerge.

Baba Muktananda said, "The scriptures and the saints have described many methods through which one can know the Self. Among these, the repetition of the mantra has been called the highest path."

There are two great mantras that express the same Truth as the *mahāvākyas.* They are *So'ham,* which means "I am That," and *Shivo'ham,* "I am Shiva," the all-pervasive, Supreme Reality. When Baba Muktananda received initiation from his Guru, Bhagawan Nityananda, these were the very words that Nityananda spoke. Baba described that moment in *Play of Consciousness,* his spiritual autobiography. "Bhagawan Nityananda said, '*Shivo'ham,*... this is how it should be.' And this great, supreme, and radiant mantra of Parashiva destroyed the innumerable sounds that had been rising in the space within my heart since time without end, making me wander through endless births and rebirths."

So'ham. Shivo'ham. Become steadfast in this great Truth. To be steadfast in knowledge is to hold the key to the hearts of all. In the *Bhagavad Gītā,* Lord Krishna says:

> *īśhvaraḥ sarvabhūtānāṃ hṛiddeśhe 'rjuna tiṣhṭhati*
>
> The Lord abides in the hearts of all beings, O Arjuna. [18:61]

The heart is the abode of the Truth. When you want to receive knowledge, you have to enter that inner space. Whether you are repeating the mantra and want to experience the truth that it embodies, whether you are reading a book, studying a scripture, or listening to a talk, you cannot grasp spiritual knowledge through the intellect alone. The intellect as you know it must be purified. Then wisdom arises from deep within the great space of the heart.

Our lives, says the *Bhagavad Gītā,* are governed and bound by three different qualities, or *gunas.* These are the basic attributes of nature, which determine the inherent characteristics of all created beings. They are *sattva*, the quality of purity, light, harmony, and goodness; *rajas*, the quality of activity or passion; and *tamas*, the quality of inertia, darkness, and ignorance.

Throughout the day, a person experiences all of these different qualities at one time or another. At one moment you may feel very pure, light, and harmonious, in touch with the goodness of your heart. That is *sattva*. At another moment you feel full of activity, full of desire for one thing or another, full of differences. That is *rajas*. At yet another time you feel so lazy, so dull; it is as if you are living in a dungeon. That is *tamas*. All people go through these different phases because of the *gunas*. They color everything you do.

Lord Krishna also describes three kinds of knowledge, each associated with a different *guna*. His descriptions are very vivid and easy to recognize. This is what He says about the knowledge which is colored by *tamoguna*, the quality of darkness:

> *yat-tu kṛitsnavad ekasmin-kārye saktam ahaitukam /*
> *atattvārthavad-alpaṃ cha tat-tāmasam-udāhṛitam //*

> That knowledge which is attached to one single effect
> as if it were the whole, without reason,
> without foundation in truth, and trivial,
> that is declared to be tamasic. [18:22]

In Maharashtra, in India, there was a poet-saint named Jnaneshwar, which literally means the lord of knowledge, the master of all knowledge. Though he lived a very short time on this earth, Jnaneshwar is still so loved and respected that he is always called *Mahārāj* and honored as the king of yogis. The commentary that he wrote on the *Bhagavad Gītā* is also called by his name, the *Jñāneshwarī*. In it, the poet-saint comments on this verse very eloquently. We really must be grateful to him for this, because the *shlokas*, the verses, of the *Bhagavad Gītā* can be quite abstruse. So, Jnaneshwar Maharaj very compassionately explains the form of knowledge governed by the darkness of *tamoguna*, saying:

To call this knowledge would be as irrelevant as saying that the eyes of a blind man are large,

That the ears of a deaf man are well-shaped, or that filthy water is good to drink. In the same way, tamasic knowledge is knowledge in name only.

O Arjuna, this kind of knowledge wanders naked, unclothed by scriptural authority, turning its back on tradition.

This knowledge, possessed by the evil spirit of darkness, spins around like a madman.

It regards no person as a friend, nor any food as prohibited. It is like a dog let loose in a deserted village,

Which eats everything, leaving aside only what its mouth cannot reach, or what is so hot it will burn its tongue.

Just as everything is food for death, and as all things are fuel for fire, in the same way, the quality of darkness considers the whole world as its own possession.

A man with this understanding cannot reach beyond the idea that the body is the Self and that a stone image is the Supreme.

All that the physical eyes can see and all that pleases the senses is the only real experience, as far as he is concerned.

When your knowledge is colored by *tamoguna*, it is very dark. You may think you have understood the teachings. However, if your understanding is covered by darkness, it does you no good. You do not have the ability to translate what you have heard or read into your daily actions, and you are subject to delusions. *Tamoguna*. Therefore, right in the beginning Jnaneshwar Maharaj says this cannot even be called knowledge. Knowledge is pure, it is profound. Knowledge is liberating. When you attain *jñāna-vyavasthiti*, steadfastness in the knowledge of the Self, you experience liberation, the goal of life. There are people who think they have understood the teaching, but then they also ask, "Why don't I have the same high experiences that other people do?" It is because their knowledge is colored by darkness.

What does this really mean? They use knowledge for their own selfish ends. It is said even wicked people can quote the scriptures.

People quote the *Bhagavad Gītā*, they quote the Bible, they quote the *Guru Gītā*, whether they believe in these scriptures or not. That is tamasic knowledge. It will not bear fruit. There are people who use the teachings to make money. When the teachings are nothing but a livelihood for you, a way to earn a few slices of bread, that is also tamasic knowledge. There is no purity in it at all. So, Jnaneshwar Maharaj says, such learning has no scriptural value: "It should not be regarded as knowledge but as the eyes of darkness."

Some people take a bit of wisdom, a little piece of the teachings, back home and use it as a weapon to browbeat their families. That is another way to abuse the profound power of the teachings. Baba said, "You don't have to make a great display of your yoga. Nor do you have to dump your knowledge on your dear ones. Love them more. Repeat the mantra quietly and clear your mind so that when they speak to you, you can also experience more of their love." That is sattvic knowledge, pure knowledge.

Knowledge is not something that resides exclusively in the brain, making your head bigger and bigger. Every bit of you matters. Every cell in your body matters. Everything you feel and do matters. When your knowledge is pure, you are functioning from the deepest part of your being, from the great heart where the Truth abides. In tamasic knowledge there is no compassion and, therefore, no support from the scriptures either.

Jnaneshwar Maharaj says:

> Now I have explained to you tamasic knowledge, which has the quality of darkness, so you may know it and reject it.

In the *Bhagavad Gītā*, Lord Krishna describes rajasic knowledge next. He says:

pṛithaktvena tu yaj-jñānaṃ nānābhāvān-pṛithagvidhān /
vetti sarveṣhu bhūteṣhu taj-jñānaṃ viddhi rājasam //

That knowledge which sees all beings
as separate entities of various kinds,
each different from the other,
know that knowledge to be rajasic. [18:21]

Jnaneshwar Maharaj comments on this, saying:

> Listen, O Arjuna. The knowledge which is bound by the idea of separateness is rajasic.
>
> Just as a child is unable to recognize gold disguised in the form of ornaments, similarly, through rajasic knowledge, the inherent oneness of all things is concealed in names and forms.
>
> Just as an ignorant person doesn't recognize clay after it has been made into pots and jars, as fire is invisible in a bright light,
>
> As a foolish person doesn't distinguish threads if they are woven into cloth, or as a dull person hates the canvas on which a picture is painted,
>
> In the same way, because of rajasic knowledge, created objects appear to be separate and the perception of unity is obscured.
>
> Then, just as fire seems to be separate in different logs, just as fragrance seems distinct in different flowers, and as a separate moon seems to be reflected in every pool of water,
>
> In the same way, rajasic knowledge perceives multiplicity in created things and distinguishes them as large and small.

Rajasic knowledge continually sees differences. It only sees separateness. From its perspective, the individual soul and the Supreme Soul appear to be two entirely different things. This is the knowledge of duality. Once again, when your mind hasn't become clear, when you are not sure of your path, you are forever flirting with rajasic knowledge. You are not entirely sure whether you will benefit from spiritual practices or not. You are not one hundred percent sure whether meditation is going to bear the right fruit... in the right proportion... at the right time. Or, anyway, not absolutely positively the fruit you want.

In *rajoguna*, you are constantly making distinctions. "This must be good, but not that. This must be wonderful, but that sounds terrible to me." You spend your time creating differences. "Maybe I should only repeat the mantra and not chant the *Guru Gītā*. Maybe I should only do seva and never go to a program... Or is it the other way around?" You are forever wondering if one thing is better than another, and you apply the same kind of rajasic thought process to all your interactions with people. "Hmmm. They are saying that now, but yesterday they said this, and what will they be saying the day after tomorrow? Hmmm. What does it *mean?*" Never actually going into the heart, the great space, but only remaining on the surface of daily life.

Rajasic knowledge: not knowing that the light of the moon and the light of the sun are the same; not recognizing that it is one moon being reflected in many ponds; not understanding that one God dwells in everyone's heart.

Sometimes people used to come up to Baba Muktananda and ask him how he could possibly love everyone equally. Baba would laugh and ask them, "Why not?" They would protest vehemently. "No, *no*, Baba, listen. How can you love all people with the same intensity?" And Baba would laugh and say, "Why shouldn't I?" Then they would turn to the translator. "Can you please translate correctly? Baba! How is it possible for you not to hate at least one person?"

Of course, Baba gave different answers at different times, wonderful answers from his own experience. But this is a perfect example of rajasic knowledge. Just because you haven't had the experience of loving everyone equally, you cultivate doubt and create differences.

One of the reasons the great ones can love everyone equally is that they have no selfish interest. They don't desire anyone's wealth or anyone's body or anyone's wife. There is nothing they want and they want for nothing. In this state it is possible to love everyone, because you have no regrets, you have no anger, and you have no fear. So you are able to experience love for all humankind. There is no transaction, no bargain. This is not a love of business, it is the love of God. And so, there is no duality and no separateness, but only and always the experience of oneness.

In the *Bhagavad Gītā*, Lord Krishna describes pure knowledge, sattvic knowledge, in the following way:

sarvabhūteṣhu yenaikaṃ bhāvam-avyayam-īkṣhate /
avibhaktaṃ vibhakteṣhu taj-jñānaṃ viddhi sāttvikam //

That knowledge by which one sees
the one indestructible reality in all beings,
undivided, not separate in separate beings,
know that knowledge to be sattvic. [18:20]

Jnaneshwar Maharaj comments on this, saying:

> Clear vision enables a person to see all things distinctly. Similarly, with pure knowledge he can understand the true nature of things.
>
> O Arjuna, through the development of sattvic knowledge, the knower and the known merge into one.
>
> The sun can never see darkness, the ocean doesn't know rivers separately, and no one can embrace his own shadow.
>
> It is the same with this knowledge, for through it all creation, from the highest gods to a blade of grass, is seen to be one.
>
> A picture cannot be seen by feeling it, salt cannot be washed with water, and dreams do not occur after waking.
>
> Similarly, the knower, the known, and the process of knowing cease to exist separately when one understands them with the help of this knowledge.
>
> An intelligent person doesn't melt down gold ornaments to see whether they are made of gold, or strain waves to get water.

I love that image! Have you ever tried to do that, strain waves to get water? It is a wonderful analogy for something that almost everyone does. Jnaneshwar Maharaj continues:

> In the same way, sattvic knowledge is beyond the perception which sees differences in things.
>
> If a person happens to look in a mirror, he sees his own image. Similarly, when the knower knows himself, the known disappears.
>
> Pure knowledge is a storehouse of the wealth of liberation.

Sattvic knowledge is what Lord Krishna invokes in chapter sixteen when he describes the divine virtues to Arjuna. We have talked about becoming steadfast in yoga. This is another aspect of it that is just as important to cultivate. Become steadfast in knowledge. Even in a troublesome time, use the purest knowledge to understand what is happening. When your emotions are going haywire, instead of playing one emotion off against another, use *jnana*, pure knowledge, and try to understand your feelings in that way.

When you repeat the mantra, you are in touch with sattvic knowledge. The pure vibrations of the mantra bring you to it. When you are sitting in meditation, when you allow your mind to become still and your breath to become deep, when all the impulses of the body have quieted down and you experience the great silence at the center of your being, know that you are in touch with true knowledge. It is your own. Become steadfast in that.

Eleven years ago, Baba made a pilgrimage to Kashmir to visit the sacred places where the sages meditated and became steadfast in knowledge. A few days before Baba's arrival, one of the dignitaries of Kashmir was assassinated. His son came for Baba's darshan. He implored Baba to visit his father's grave and bring peace to his soul.

Baba arrived there at sunset. He stood before the tomb in the golden twilight and sang one verse from the Upanishads over and over again. There was such depth and beauty in his voice. Each syllable of that verse came to life.

Every time I think of this verse, I remember how moved I was when Baba chanted it that day, and I contemplate the extraordinary blessing he gave to that departed soul. Just a few months before that, I had taken *sannyāsa*, the vows of monkhood. During that ceremony, Baba also sang the same verse quietly, many, many times. The verse is from the *Īshāvāsya Upanishad*, and it goes like this:

īśhāvāsyaṃ-idaṃ sarvaṃ yat-kiñ-cha jagatyāṃ jagat /
tena tyaktena bhuñjīthā mā gṛidhaḥ kasyasvid-dhanam //

Know that everything that moves in this changing world
is enveloped by God.
Therefore, find your enjoyment in renunciation
and do not covet what belongs to others.
Since God pervades everything, nothing belongs to you,
not even your own body. [1]

This is the fire of knowledge. Knowing that everything in the world is enveloped by God. Knowing that true enjoyment can only be found in *tyāga*, in renunciation, and not in possessions. Knowing how to be content with what happens to you, inside and out, and not going after what others have.

When you have this, when this knowledge arises inside you through the grace of the Guru, you do understand that everything is God, and you need not worry, you need not fear. You are only a caretaker of God's wealth, in whatever form it takes, whether it is your body, your mind, your ego, your intellect, the possessions you have outside, or the virtues you have inside. All that is, is God's. Once your understanding has become so steadfast and so pure, you know that you are simply taking care of all these things, seen and unseen, known and unknown, for God. Then you don't have the terrible attachment which brings about pain. Then your freedom is complete.

This is the kind of knowledge in which you must become established, unwavering and steadfast. This is the knowledge of the Self.

With great respect and great love, I welcome you all with all my heart.

July 11, 1993

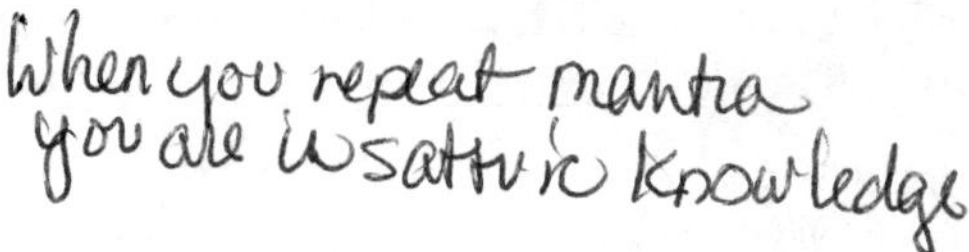

When you repeat mantra
you are in sattvic knowledge

Anger is worst enemy cause it is linked w/ unending chain of desires.

You have to look @ it, analyze it, learn to dissolve it - then you become disciplined

Whenever there is dissatisfaction there is anger and there it leads you into unfullfilled desires ~~once~~ again.

To be disciplined = a truly happy person

To establish control over your cravings

To be disciplined doesn't mean being bossiness - but to be watchful of how the process begins and FOCUS on what is arising and what subsides, to see the seeds of anger and desires start to grow w/o following them wherever they lead to.

CHAPTER FIVE

FREEDOM FROM ANGER

PART 1

~

Akrodha

WITH GREAT RESPECT AND GREAT LOVE, I welcome you all with all my heart.

This is the summer of virtues, the summer of great qualities. In every program, before we begin to contemplate the virtues discussed in the *Bhagavad Gītā*, we chant. Chanting is a feast. To chant, you need no virtues. All you have to do is give yourself to the sound. It doesn't matter what you are feeling in the beginning. You can just chant and experience the exquisite delight that is the nature of the supreme Self. However, the rest of the time, you do need to cultivate virtues. You need their support.

In the Chinese philosophy of Taoism, the sage of the *Tao Te Ching* asks a series of beautiful questions about virtue:

> Can you coax your mind from its wandering and keep to
> the original oneness?
> Can you let your body become supple as a newborn child's?
> Can you cleanse your inner vision until you see nothing but
> the light?
> Can you love people and lead them without imposing your will?

Can you deal with the most vital matters by letting events take their course?
Can you step back from your own mind, and thus understand all things?

Tonight, we are going to look at the virtue called *akrodha*, freedom from anger. In the *Bhagavad Gītā*, the Lord says:

kāma eṣha krodha eṣha rajoguṇa-samudbhavaḥ /
mahāśhano mahāpāpmā viddhyenam-iha vairiṇam //

It is desire; it is anger,
born of the quality of *rajas*,
all-devouring, greatly sinful.
Know this as the enemy here, in this world. [3:37]

In other words, the worst enemy you have on earth can be found in the dark corners of your own mind. Desire and anger. Where there is one, the other is not far behind. When a desire is thwarted or denied, it turns into anger. However much people like to think they are provoked, a person's anger is always his own creation. Truly, if you get angry, you have no one to blame but yourself. "Can you coax your mind from its wandering and keep to the original oneness?" Perhaps that is why, when the mind is out of control, people often say, "I lost it."

The sources of anger may appear to be mysterious. For instance, sometimes a person is speaking to you. What he or she is saying is very nice, very good, very true. Nevertheless, all of a sudden, out of the blue, you start feeling uncentered, unsettled. Something is not sitting well with you, but you can't tell what it is. You keep listening. Whatever is being said is fine. And yet…

There are several distinct possibilities for your discomfort. For example, the person may be saying something pleasant or kind in words, but feeling very agitated inside and sending that energy out. Or it may be that this person did or said something to you a long time ago that was never resolved. And now, even though you may not even be aware of it, the memory kicks in. It may be the furthest thing from your mind, consciously, and still it is the source of your uneasiness. Or, maybe, in a past lifetime—if you believe in such things—this person caused you harm, and to this day, in *karmāshaya*, the reservoir of karmas in your being, you are carrying the impressions of those wrongs, those negativities, those thoughts. So this time around, out of the blue, this bit of old karma is triggered and you experience a disturbance that appears to be unwarranted, inappropriate. You experience a sort of churning, even though what this person is saying appears to be quite nice, full of goodness, perfectly wonderful.

The origin of your anger may be quite complicated. Still, one thing is very clear and simple. You have got to stop the cycle somewhere. If you begin right now, there is hope. On the other hand, if you don't deal with this, if you just let the negativities subside for the time being, it will only get worse. These feelings will never leave you on their own; they will age right along with you. They will follow you from one lifetime to the next. Therefore, the yogic scriptures say, you must look at your anger, you must analyze it and learn to dissolve it. Anger is the worst of the inner enemies, because of its connection to the unending chain of desire. Whenever there is dissatisfaction, there is anger. Wherever there is one desire, there is also bound to be another.

Once a *sadhu*, a wandering yogi, was sitting on the bank of a river. It was a lovely afternoon, not too hot, not too cold. The sadhu had spent a very beautiful morning, just the sort he loved. He had bathed in a clear stream, said his prayers, and performed his spiritual practices in a fragrant forest, under a shady tree. Then he had eaten very well in the kitchen of a wealthy man, who had a pious cook. The cook had heaped the sadhu's plate full, two or three times in a row, and sent him on his way with a basket full of tasty things to eat for supper. Now, here he was, on the bank of a pretty stream, completely satisfied from head to toe. Truly, there was nothing left to desire—except perhaps for a tiny nap. Just a tiny little nap.

The sadhu's eyelids began to get heavy and flutter lazily like butterflies drinking honey. Just as he was about to doze off, he saw a washerman come walking down the bank in his direction, leading two donkeys loaded with dirty clothes. The sadhu thought, "Oh, I hope he doesn't come here. I am in no mood for small talk... and he must smell awful. All those dirty clothes, those dirty donkeys." The sadhu quickly closed his eyes so that the washerman would think he was asleep.

But the washerman was a washerman. He was a free being, much freer than the sadhu, in fact. He called out, "Hey, babaji! I need to go back home and get something I forgot. Could you watch my donkeys while I'm gone? Please, you're a holy man! You should be helping humanity. I'll be back soon."

The sadhu pretended not to hear. He just sat there under the tree with his eyes closed, hoping the man would go away, and sure enough, his prayer was answered. He heard footsteps walking away and he dozed off sweetly in the shade.

When the sadhu woke up, an hour had passed and the washerman was back, shouting, *screaming*, as he came up the hill toward him. "Where are my donkeys?" The washerman's face was red as a beet, and he was directing all this rage at the sadhu. "You were supposed to look after my donkeys. Why didn't you do it? You're a sadhu! You go find my donkeys and bring them back!"

There is an old saying: When a man is wrong and won't admit it, he always gets angry. And that is exactly what happened to the sadhu. He became absolutely furious. "This is no way to treat a man of God," he shouted back. "You are supposed to speak to me with respect. Hey! Don't you kick me! I am not one of your donkeys!"

"I know!" the washerman said. "My donkeys have more sense!" And they began to fight.

What a day the sadhu was having—from a lunch fit for a king to a fistfight in the dirt with a crude, foul-smelling washerman. What a fall. He tried holding the man off, but then, you know what happens... he lost his temper.

Now the washerman was very healthy and strong from all the exercise he got washing clothes, and the sadhu, who never got any exercise at all, was very skinny and frail. In no time at all, the washerman had him pinned to the ground and was pummeling him with both fists. Eventually, just as the person who takes a beating gets tired, the one giving the beating also wears himself out. Soon, both men were lying in the mud, completely exhausted.

After a few minutes, the sadhu stood up and began to dab water on his aching body. The poor man had lost his state of serenity, as well as the fight. The only thing he had not lost was his anger. But where could he direct it now? He was done with the washerman and there was no one else in sight.

So the sadhu raised his eyes toward heaven and cried, "O God! I have been worshiping You all my life! I think of You, I pray to You, I adore You. For the past thirty years, God, not a single day, not a single night has gone by that I haven't thought of You. For Your sake, Lord, I have given up all the comforts of life. I sleep under a *tree!* O Lord, most of the time I don't even get enough to eat. I live on berries! All this I have done for You. But when I needed You, O God, where were You?"

It is said, when you are in trouble, if God doesn't help you, then He is in trouble. So the sadhu wanted to know where God was when the washerman was sitting on his chest.

As soon as the sadhu babaji stopped complaining, a voice boomed out of heaven, "O sadhu, I wanted to help so much. I came as soon as you called. And I would have saved you, I would have pulled you out of there with My own hands. But when I looked down, all I saw was a tangled mass of angry energy. I couldn't tell who was the washerman and who was the sadhu."

This is exactly what happens. Once anger erupts, you can't tell who is right and who is wrong, who is a good person and who is not. Anger takes over. It doesn't just take over one aspect of your being, either; anger takes the whole thing. Nor can you hide anger somewhere deep inside, where no one else can see it. If that's what you think, you're making a big mistake. Anger oozes out of every part of your body, except your awareness. So everyone can see it but you. You may walk around with the idea that you are projecting an image that is very positive, very wonderful, very yogic; but if anger has made a home in the cells of your body, it shows.

Freedom from anger is a magnificent virtue. Once again, to experience it, you have to go through layer after layer after layer of memory and association, but this happens naturally, with each practice that you perform. For example, every morning we chant the *Guru Gītā* together. Each recitation of the *Guru Gītā* will put an end to one cell of anger in your body. It really does. It purifies your whole system. Every spiritual practice you perform removes a bit of the stigma of anger.

So, in the *Bhagavad Gītā*, Lord Krishna says,

> *śhaknotīhaiva yaḥ soḍhuṃ prāk-śharīravimokṣhaṇāt /*
> *kāmakrodhodbhavaṃ vegaṃ sa yuktaḥ sa sukhī naraḥ //*

> He who is able to endure, here on earth,
> before liberation from the body,
> the agitation that arises from desire and anger,
> is disciplined;
> truly he is a happy man. [5:23]

When are you truly happy? When you can dissolve a desire before it gathers you up in the cycle that turns into anger, when you can catch the seed of a desire and roast it at will, then you become a very happy person. In yoga, this is what is meant by discipline: establishing control over your own cravings. Many people hear this and say, "What can I do? I am the way I am." If you are saying this from the highest perspective, then it is part of a great and true philosophy of being. "I am that I am." But if you are saying this because you are collapsing under a stack of desires, caught between layers of hard cold anger, then you are doomed. "What can I do? I'm helpless. That's the way I am." You are simply letting your impulses and emotions run your life without making any effort to control them.

A person who does nothing about his anger spends his life in hell. Hell is nothing but living in your own negativities, your own bad mind. It can be very subtle. You may think you are only having good, kind thoughts. Meanwhile, a dark undercurrent of anger runs through everything you do. Unless you become aware of it and learn to track its movements, this hidden flow of anger is very difficult to overcome.

It can be quite embarrassing, when you think you are having nice positive thoughts and feelings, to discover that, underneath, there is a lot of agitation. Some part of you is looking for a chance to get back at someone; in fact, you are really angry; secretly you are fuming about something that happened. Unfailingly, such a thing exists because it has not been taken care of. Once it is dealt with — acknowledged, examined, and released — it dissolves forever.

Most of the time, however, people would rather not take care of it. This is obvious in the way they lead their lives. When most people experience pain, their main concern is to get over it. They want to reach the other end of the tunnel as quickly as possible. Instead of going through the pain, experiencing it and learning something from it, they always ask themselves and others, "When will this be over?" They go to an astrologer and ask, "When will my bad times be over? Can you please tell me how long this is going to last?" Or they go to a psychic. Or they go and sit by a stream, in the hope that, if they watch it flow for a while, everything will be all right. There is a natural tendency to run away, to quit, to cop out and not face what is painful. Why don't people experience the great light inside? Why don't people experience the great delight inside? Because of the layers and layers of anger and unfulfilled desires.

Every now and then, there is a spark. A person catches a glimpse of the Truth, experiences a portion of love. However, it evaporates. Every now and then, a person becomes completely ecstatic, wants nothing more in this world, feels entirely fulfilled. However, it doesn't last. No matter what the person does, the experience does not last.

Why? Can you say "The ocean of delight within me has run dry?" No. Can you say "The ocean of delight, the eternal Self, is finished; it doesn't exist any more?" No. The ocean of delight is beyond limitation. It is always full. It is only your experience of it that comes and goes, your experience that is sporadic. Why? Because of unfulfilled desires. Your mind is constantly running after different things. Even if you get one of them, your pleasure doesn't last. And then there is always another new desire that captures your attention—and then another, and another. You can never fulfill them all, and there's no end to it.

As long as there is so much unfinished business, you will experience agitation. It is like a knife in the heart. It doesn't matter how much great knowledge you possess, how fervently you invoke the great statements of the Vedas—I am the Truth, I am Light, I am the Self—you experience this annoying agitation, this terrible acid eating you up from inside. So, Lord Krishna tells Arjuna to free himself from desire and anger.

Freedom from anger, *akrodha,* is a truly magnificent virtue. "He who is able to endure here on earth, before liberation from the body, before the body falls away, the agitation that arises from desire and anger, is disciplined." In becoming disciplined, contemplation is a very useful tool. You watch your mind, you watch what comes up. That is discipline. Discipline doesn't mean somebody ordering you around, somebody constantly saying, "Do this, do that, go here, go there, sit here, sit there." That is not discipline, it is merely a display of bossiness.

Discipline is a question of focus, of watching what arises and what subsides, being a witness, and gaining the power actually to understand the very beginnings of the process, the seeds of desire and anger. When you can trace the footsteps of anger and unfulfilled desire without being compelled to follow wherever they lead, then you are called a disciplined person, one who has acquired the power to understand himself.

The *Mahābhārata* tells a story of an ascetic named Kaushika who was meticulous in observing all the vows of purity. One day he was sitting under a tree reciting the Vedas. Unfortunately, a crane in the top branches chose that moment to relieve itself, and the whole mess landed right in the middle of Kaushika's shaved head. Kaushika looked up at the bird in fury, and his glance, filled with the power of his austerities, stopped its heart. The bird plunged through the branches and fell at his feet, dead.

Kaushika was stunned. He felt remorseful at the sight of the lifeless creature, but at the same time he couldn't help feeling impressed with himself. He had never realized how much he was attaining through his practices. So although he felt ashamed, honestly ashamed, and sorry for the crane, secretly he was also thrilled.

In that confused state of mind, he went off to beg for his dinner. Wonderful smells of food cooking drifted out of the first house he came to. As was the custom, Kaushika waited by the kitchen door for the housewife to notice him. He could see that she was busy cooking. Then her husband called from the next room, and he sounded tired and hungry. Of course, she had to go see what he wanted and then serve him his dinner. Kaushika understood that it was her dharma, her duty as a wife, to look after her household first. But his stomach was growling. After all, he was a renunciant of great attainments, and she was keeping him waiting. Besides, his anger had proved to be so powerful, he couldn't help toying with it. "She doesn't know who is on her doorstep," he thought. "She had better not make me mad."

The next moment, she saw him and came to the door with an apology on her lips. "Kind sir, how long have you been waiting? May I get you something to eat?"

Kaushika's anger exploded again. "It's about time you noticed. Do you always keep holy men waiting? Don't you know the consequences of disrespect?"

"Why are you so angry?" the woman said. "Couldn't you see my husband needed me? I am no crane, sir. You can't kill me with a violent thought."

Kaushika gasped. How did she know about the crane?

"O great one," the woman continued, "your anger is your mortal enemy. If I were you, I would go to Mithila and ask for the grace of Dharmavyada. He is a sage of steady wisdom."

Kaushika thanked the woman humbly, with folded hands. He saw her as the instrument of God. So he touched the doorstep of her house reverently, as if it were a temple, and set out at once for Mithila. He expected to find the sage living in some lonely hermitage far away from the noise and bustle of ordinary life.

Isn't it great? The mind most people have! It actually leaps to think up these fantasies about meeting the Guru. "A Guru, living in a forest all by himself... with one or two disciples..." And then, "Tigers and sheep live together in harmony there..." And "The moment you come before this great Guru, in this primeval wood, the moment he lays his eyes upon you, he says, 'My child, you have come.'" Then you visualize yourself sitting before this great being with your hands folded, your heart filled with humility, your entire spirit brimming with devotion. And, as the great Guru bestows his gracious glance upon you, you who know nothing begin to recite the scriptures.

These are the kinds of visualizations people have when they come to see a Guru. Kaushika was no different. So he also was in for a big surprise. When he arrived in the city of Mithila and asked people where Dharmavyadha lived, they didn't point to a forest; they directed him to a butcher's shop. And the butcher himself turned out to be the sage.

This was almost too much for Kaushika. He stood at a distance, trying to gather his wits, when he saw the butcher suddenly stand up and walk out of the shop, right over to him. "Reverend sir, are you all right?" said the sage respectfully. "Did that good woman give you something to eat before she sent you to me?"

Kaushika's jaw dropped. They were in cahoots!

"I know why you are here," the sage went on. "Come home with me this evening."

That night, Kaushika looked into the eyes of Dharmavyadha. They were as deep as the ocean, as clear as a mountain stream, as steady as a mountain, as pure as God's love. And then Dharmavyadha spoke to him about dharma, about living a life filled with the divine virtues. He gave Kaushika the teachings that echo throughout the *Mahābhārata:*

akīrti vinayo hanti hantyamanarthaṃ parākramaḥ /
hanti nityaṃ kṣhamā krodhāchāro hantyalakṣhaṇam //

Humility puts an end to a bad reputation,
self-effort destroys misfortune,
forgiveness dissolves anger,
and good conduct wears away undesirable qualities.

dharmo jayati nādharmaḥ satyaṃ jayati nānṛitam /
kṣhamā jayati na krodhaḥ kṣhamāvān brahmaṇo bhavet //

In the final analysis, dharma, righteousness, always wins,
never unrighteousness.
Truth is always victorious; untruth always fails in the end.
Patience, forbearance, always wins out, not anger.
One who is patient becomes established in the Absolute,
in Brahman.

Staying with the sage, Kaushika saw what true greatness was. He saw how every gesture the saint made, every word he spoke to his family, his neighbors, and the people who came into his shop was filled with love, simplicity, and God's grace. In the midst of all the turmoil of ordinary life, he had attained the state of steady wisdom.

This state is the greatest attainment. When you become free from anger, steady wisdom is the fruit. Becoming free from anger may seem like a lot of work, but it is a great task filled with joy. You get to discover yourself. You come to understand your limitations; you also understand your great glory. Every time you come across one of your limitations, such as your inability to conquer your anger, you also realize the infinite power of God's compassion, and that moves you. When you are moved by God's love, your anger dissolves. As the sage said, forgiveness dissolves anger. This means forgiving yourself as well as others, constantly having great thoughts about others and the universe, and performing your duty with your heart completely settled in it. It is very important that you give your heart to your duty. That is when it flourishes.

Whenever people asked Baba, "How do I give up anger?" Baba would answer, "Just drop it." When he said that, he also gave people the grace and the will to do it. It is a great teaching to put into practice. Just drop it. Just do it. In the process of letting go of your anger, you contemplate it, you perform self-inquiry, you transcend the layers and layers of impressions and consequences that have accumulated like a crust around your heart. They dissolve in the yogic fire of God's love.

Now, let us take a few seconds to contemplate once more the words of Chinese philosophy that we heard in the beginning. The sage Lao Tsu asked:

> Can you coax your mind from its wandering and keep to the original oneness?
> Can you let your body become supple as a newborn child's?
> Can you cleanse your inner vision until you see nothing but the light?
> Can you love people and lead them without imposing your will?

With great respect and great love, I welcome you all with all my heart.

July 31, 1993

CHAPTER SIX

FREEDOM FROM ANGER

PART 2

Akrodha

WITH GREAT RESPECT AND WITH GREAT LOVE, I welcome you all with all my heart.

Chanting is a great feast. Chanting is nectar. Baba Muktananda used to say, when you meditate for a long time all the *rasa*, the juiciness, in the body may burn up in the fire of yoga. To replenish yourself, to regenerate the cells, you need the flavor, the nectar, the sweetness, that is released in the body by chanting.

This is the magical summer of divine virtues. Seekers of knowledge have come from all over the world to participate in ashram life and embrace the daily schedule, which contains meditation, chanting, *Gurusevā* or selfless service, courses, and Intensives. All these activities inspire introspection. In fact, they demand it. Self-inquiry and the reevaluation of life are the faithful companions of spiritual practices.

Many people come here thinking they will be given everything they need. This understanding is good as long as they don't forget to participate fully in what is given to them. To hold any gift, a vessel must be strong and clean, or even nectar can be wasted. How pure and how strong must a person become, then, to hold the gift of wisdom? For this reason, a seeker must develop virtues and put them into action. Then he becomes more and more lucid, until his whole being is filled with light and he is as transparent as the wind. A vessel that pure deserves to hold the knowledge of the Self, *ātma-jñāna.*

A lot of people say they want to know the Self, the supreme Self, and they may be sincere. But they are not willing to part with their concepts, their habits, and all the old familiar patterns, however devastating these may be. They are not willing to give up the burden of the possessions, tangible and intangible, that stand in their way. This makes it very difficult to hear the Truth, to see the Truth, to know the Truth and to live the Truth.

This is precisely the reason for spending time in the ashram: to learn to open your hand and let go of everything that binds you, so that you are free to take hold of what you really want. Shirdi Sai Baba used to say, "I give people what they want in the hope that one day they will come to want what I have to give."

At times it may seem that some people are going around the ashram doing whatever they like, putting their own physical comfort before everything else. Truly speaking, these people are just being given a certain amount of leeway. Little by little they grow accustomed to the practices until, one day, they become acutely aware of their own longing. Then they can begin to receive the knowledge of the Self.

Spending time in the ashram is a great sadhana. It is not an overnight trip, a brief stopover, where you pick up your ticket for knowledge of the Self and then continue to revolve in the cycle of birth and death. The ashram is the place for you to take a good look at the bundle of your actions and clean the mirror of your mind. Your *own* mind—you don't have to do it for others. So, the ashram is a wonderful place for sadhana.

We have begun to unravel the mystery of *akrodha*, freedom from anger, absence of anger, renunciation of anger. As you may remember, in chapter three of the *Bhagavad Gītā*, Lord Krishna tells Arjuna that anger is one of the most destructive tendencies in a human being, and freedom from anger, one of the greatest virtues. Very pointedly, Lord Krishna says:

kāma eṣha krodha eṣha rajoguṇa-samudbhavaḥ /
mahāśhano mahāpāpmā viddhyenam-iha vairiṇam //

This force is desire, this force is anger;
its source is the *rajoguna.*
Voracious and greatly sinful,
know this to be the enemy here in this world. [3:37]

As soon as people hear they must renounce their desire and their anger in order to attain the highest state, they become quite agitated. For some reason, people want to believe they can ascend to the realm of supreme Truth with all their unresolved stuff intact.

In this verse the Lord says that desire and anger are born of *rajas.* What does He mean? You have heard that the universe is made up of three *gunas,* three qualities: *sattva* (purity), *rajas* (activity), and *tamas* (inertia). They are like the three strands of a rope. They are the threads that make up the fabric of reality. A human being, too, is composed of these three qualities: *sattva, rajas,* and *tamas.* Every thought, every word, every feeling, every gesture, and every action is prompted by these three modifications. They color everything we think, feel, say, and do.

Lord Krishna expounds upon these three qualities at some length, and the great saint of Maharashtra, Jnaneshwar Maharaj, elucidates them further in his inspired commentary on the *Bhagavad Gītā* called *Jñāneshwarī.* Listen to these descriptions very carefully. Lord Krishna says to Arjuna:

sattvaṃ rajas-tama iti guṇāḥ prakṛitisambhavāḥ /
nibadhnanti mahābāho dehe dehinam-avyayam //

Sattva, rajas, tamas,
thus, the qualities born of nature,
bind fast in the body, O Arjuna,
the indestructible embodied Self. [14:5]

Jnaneshwar Maharaj comments:

> These three qualities are called purity, passion, and darkness, and they are born of matter.

> Of these three, purity is the highest, passion is intermediate, and darkness is the lowest.
>
> These three qualities are inherent in all our mental tendencies, just as the three stages of childhood, youth, and old age are inherent in the body.
>
> As soon as the great Self enters the body as the Knower of the field, he identifies with the body.

As you listen to Jnaneshwar's descriptions of the three qualities, try to relate them to your life, see if you can understand how they affect every thought you think and every action you perform; see how they affect you in your waking state, your dream state, and even the state of deep sleep.

In the *Bhagavad Gītā*, Lord Krishna continues:

> *tatra sattvaṃ nirmalatvāt prakāśhakam-anāmayam /*
> *sukhasañgena badhnāti jñānasañgena chānagha //*

> Of these, *sattva*, because it is free from impurity,
> illuminating, and free from disease,
> binds a man by attachment to happiness
> and by attachment to knowledge, O Arjuna. [14:6]

Understand, Lord Krishna is saying that even *sattva*, the quality of purity, is an attachment. It is an attachment to happiness, to knowledge, or even to purity itself. Jnaneshwar Maharaj comments:

> A man becomes excited by his knowledge, destroys his happiness, and ends by casting aside the joy of Self-realization (*ātma sākshātkāra*).
>
> He rejoices in learning, delights in recognition, and boasts that he has everything he wants.
>
> He says to himself, "How fortunate I am! My happiness is unrivaled!"
>
> He is puffed up with the various modifications of goodness.
>
> He is bound by the evil spirit of the pride of learning.
>
> He feels no sorrow at losing the understanding that he embodies spiritual light, and his knowledge of worldly affairs becomes as vast as the heavens.

He masters all worldly knowledge, understands all about sacrifices, and even knows what happens in heaven.

That is true, isn't it? These days even the rockets go there.

Then he boasts that no one is learned except him, and that his mind is the sky in which the moon of wisdom shines.

In this way, purity drives the individual soul with the reins of happiness and knowledge, just as a beggar leads his bull.

Lord Krishna continues in the *Bhagavad Gītā*:

rajo rāgātmakaṃ viddhi tṛiṣhṇāsaṅga-samudbhavam /
tan-nibadhnāti kaunteya karmasaṅgena dehinam //

Know that the quality of *rajas* is characterized by passion,
arising from thirst and attachment.
This binds a man fast, O Arjuna,
by an attachment to action. [14:7]

Jnaneshwar Maharaj explains this very beautifully too:

When desire is aroused, sense objects are thought to be sweet, although they are tinged with pain. Even the glory of Indra, the ruler of the celestial world, cannot satisfy desire.

Desire becomes so intense that even if a person possessed a mountain of gold, it would only urge him on to acquire more.

If he spends all that he has today, he is concerned about tomorrow, so he embarks on great undertakings.

A person is ready to throw away his life for even the smallest gain, and he thinks he has attained his goal if he gets a blade of grass.

O Arjuna, just as at the end of the hot season the wind is never still, similarly such a man never stops working by day or by night.

He plunges into the fire of action in pursuit of profit in heaven or on earth.

The Self, though different from the body, binds itself with the chains of desires and bears around its neck the burden of worldly affairs.

The second quality, *rajas*, or *rajoguna*, in which the attachment to actions predominates, is not difficult to understand. This one sentence explains it all: "When desire is aroused, sense objects are thought to be sweet, although they are tinged with pain." There is a moment when a young child becomes a teenager, somewhere around the age of twelve or thirteen, when a strong desire arises for another body, for another person. You can take this one example of how desire drives a person crazy. The boy or girl in this case doesn't really understand what is happening; it is just an unnamed desire. Nevertheless, this is a force that can drive a person to his or her downfall.

Lord Krishna continues:

tamas-tv-ajñānajaṃ viddhi mohanaṃ sarvadehinām /
pramādālasya-nidrābhis-tan-nibadhnāti bhārata //

Know indeed that the quality of *tamas* is born of ignorance,
which confuses all embodied beings.
This binds a man fast, O Arjuna,
with negligence, indolence, and sleepiness. [14:8]

This is *tamoguna*, the dark quality. Jnaneshwar Maharaj comments on this verse, saying:

> The veil of darkness which dulls earthly life is like the black clouds of the night of infatuation.
>
> It is the essence of ignorance; because of this alone the world dances in delusion.
>
> Lack of discrimination is its magical charm. It is a cup filled with the wine of folly, and it acts as a weapon which numbs a person's capacity to experience the Self.
>
> O Arjuna, the nature of darkness is that it securely binds anyone who identifies with the body.
>
> The only desire of his heart is for sleep; even the bliss of heaven would give him less pleasure than falling asleep.
>
> If he should lie down while walking along the road, he wouldn't even care for nectar. He would only want to sleep.
>
> If he were ever compelled to work, he would fly into a rage.

He doesn't know when or how to act, with whom or how to speak, or what he is able or unable to do.

He recklessly performs improper actions and delights in doing the wrong thing.

Tamoguna is inaction.

In this way darkness is the force of lethargy, laziness, and negligence, which binds the originally pure and free soul.

The three qualities: *sattva*, *rajas*, and *tamas*. In the *Bhagavad Gītā*, Lord Krishna continues:

sattvaṃ sukhe sañjayati rajaḥ karmaṇi bhārata /
jñānam-āvṛitya tu tamaḥ pramāde sañjayaty-uta //

The quality of *sattva* causes attachment to happiness,
and *rajas*, attachment to action;
tamas, obscuring knowledge,
causes an attachment to negligence. [14:9]

These three qualities run everybody's life. The whole purpose of yoga is to rise above them, to cleanse yourself completely and free yourself from *sattva*, *rajas*, and *tamas*. The nature of the three *gunas* explains why you think the way you think, and why you feel, speak, and act as you do. This is the entire map. There is nothing more to know, really. Sometimes your life is filled with purity. Sometimes it is mixed, as in *rajoguna*. At other times, it is densely packed, thick with impurities, and that is *tamoguna*.

By hearing the nature of these three qualities, you have at least a faint idea of what Lord Krishna means when He says that desire and anger are born of *rajoguna*. Since *rajoguna* sits between the intense purity of *sattva* and the impenetrable darkness of *tamas*, it can be confusing. *Rajoguna* is both pure and impure; it is a mixture of *sattva guna* and *tamoguna*. So, for example, when you have a desire, you justify it by saying, "But this desire will take me to the goal. I need it! I won't be able to function otherwise." Pure and impure. Or when you get angry, you may justify it by saying something like "I've got to get angry; otherwise, I cannot keep my department running on schedule." So you think that anger is the fuel to run your office or your work, and that desire is the fuel to run your life.

Depending which way your head is tilting, either toward *sattva guna* or *tamoguna*, you swing back and forth like a pendulum. You want to keep the company of the Truth but all you're doing is marking time. This confusion is basic to the nature of *rajoguna*, which is characterized by the attachment to actions.

A true seeker of knowledge will pursue the path of dharma, of right action, at any cost. He is determined to reach the highest goal, and nothing can deflect him. However, not everybody is endowed with such intense longing for God, for liberation. Most people are quite happy with the complexities of their lives. They like getting lost in the labyrinth of their actions. In fact, they love it.

All they want, every now and then, when they have gotten themselves into a terrible pickle, is for somebody to come and clear the mess away. If they happen to be sunk in a stupor, then they want somebody to come along and wake them up. If they happen to be caught in a patch of wild bushes, surrounded by thorns, they want somebody to come and cut them loose and then leave them alone. In all these cases, they want you to save them . . . and then go home.

So most people are thoroughly comfortable with the state of their own affairs. They're fond of all their delusions. If you ask them to change, you're basically going against the grain; you're rubbing them the wrong way and creating a bit of distress in their lives.

Nobody wants to go to heaven if it means leaving his familiar depressing surroundings. The force of habit is just like gravity: it holds everyone down. Since this is the case, what can we do? The best way to answer this question is with a story.

One day, a great saint of India named Tulsidas was bathing in the Ganges and he saw a scorpion swept along in the current, his little legs flailing pitifully in an effort to stay afloat. The sight filled Tulsidas with pity. So he fished the scorpion out of the water. It bit him very hard and slid off his hand back into the water, where it bobbed along, flailing, looking as if it were going to drown any moment. Again, Tulsidas picked the scorpion up, and again, it bit him. This happened ten times in a row.

"Hey!" a man standing on the bank cried out to him. Tulsidas turned around. The fellow said, "What kind of a person are you? I've been watching you trying to rescue that worthless scorpion for ten minutes. No matter how many times it stings you, you keep trying to save its life. Why don't you just let it drown?"

Tulsidas replied, "Brother, even with its life at stake, the scorpion can't go against its own nature. Why should I go against mine?"

This is the answer for us. It is our nature to seek the Truth, no matter how often we get stung or blown about in the ocean of worldly life. Let us continue the practices. They make us able to hold knowledge. They polish this vessel until it shines with the love of God. Since desire and anger are deadly enemies of the highest attainment, a true seeker must make every effort to pull desire out by the roots and extinguish the flames of anger. Baba Muktananda said, "You can expel anger from your heart through right understanding, through making yourself aware of its possible consequences, through making yourself conscious of the fact that anger will burn up all your *tapasya*, all the merits of your austerities."

The knowers of the Truth continually warn seekers about the effects of anger. In fact, there are many great stories about this. It is said, no matter how many austerities you have performed, the slightest spark of anger reduces all your merits to dust and you have to start all over again. It is said, no matter how pure a life you lead, no matter how many pure actions and thoughts fill your days, if there is even a spark of anger alive in your heart, all that purity burns in an instant.

You can observe this in your own life. You can actually watch the way unfulfilled desires turn, little by little, into sour anger. Sooner or later, it flares up. Sharp remarks, tantrums, and bitterness — all these things alienate you from your loved ones and from the things you have earned, from the knowledge you have acquired, and worst of all, from your own Self.

Anger cuts you off from your own joy, nourishment, sweetness, attainment, love. It is as if you are stranded, isolated from your deeper feelings and your true nature. Anger makes the glory of the Self, your own Self, feel like a memory from the distant past.

Therefore, a good person, a noble person, a sadhu, tries to hold his anger in check. One day, through the power of the great Self and the benefits of spiritual practice, it will dissolve.

In the *Mahābhārata* it is said:

> Six kinds of people are always miserable:
> those who are envious of others,
> those who hate others,
> those who are discontented,
> those who live on others' fortunes,
> those who are suspicious,
> and those who are angry.

In reality, it is anger that produces the other five conditions. There are many people here, in this hall and around the world, who want to bring about peace on earth. So many people offer a symbol of world peace in darshan—a white flag or a certain flower. In fact, when we went to Mexico last spring, a group of people came to the evening program. They introduced themselves as a network of peacemakers. They had a particular symbol that they wanted to offer, and they had a special song they wanted to sing. Like many people, they want to bring peace to the world. Think about this. How can you bring peace to the world when you're harboring angry thoughts?

How can you expect others to be sweet when your speech is bitter? How can you expect others to be open with you when you hang on to old resentments? How can you expect others to trust you when you are constantly being nasty behind their backs? How can you expect others to treat you kindly when you blow up at the drop of a hat? How can you expect others to love you innocently when you take offense at everything they do? How can you expect others to confide in you when you are always grouchy?

Do you see how many forms anger can take? Constant irritation, vexation, annoyance, animosity, sullenness, gruffness, outbursts, rage, bearing grudges—to name just a few—all these things are different faces of anger.

Basically, anger is a trick you play on yourself and others, to get your own way. Think about it. In your own life. Don't think about others. Leave them alone. In your own life, when have you gotten angry? Why did you get angry? How did you get angry? What did you use the anger for? How did it bear fruit?

We all begin as children, don't we? When we don't get our own way, we are angry. The moment we are angry, our parents say, "Oh, yes, yes, yes... anything you want, dear."

And we think, "Ahh. It works."

So it begins as soon as we take birth in this world; you discover that you can get angry. Crying is another form of anger. Sobbing is another form of anger. You cry and get your own way. Don't think this kind of crying is a sign of weakness. These tears are the strength of anger.

On the spiritual path getting your own way is not what will bring you liberation. Liberation comes when you find God's way and follow it.

Why even go that far, truly speaking? When you use your anger to get your own way, it doesn't make you happy, either. You end up more miserable than you were before. There is nothing worse than a person who passes his anger off as self-righteous indignation about the state of the world. This kind of anger can't help anybody because it is based on irresponsibility. People like this are always willing to blame everyone else for what is wrong in their lives, including God, but they rarely cast a cold eye on their own actions. You would be amazed how far they will go to avoid taking responsibility for the things they say, let alone the things they do. Have you noticed? No one wants to change his own actions, filled with *rajoguna, tamoguna* and *sattva guna*. They want the world to change instead.

In the *Bhagavad Gītā* Lord Krishna says:

ahaṃkāraṃ balaṃ darpaṃ kāmaṃ krodhaṃ parigraham /
vimuchya nirmamaḥ śhānto brahmabhūyāya kalpate //

Relinquishing egotism, force, arrogance,
desire, anger, and possession of property;
unselfish, tranquil, a man is fit
for oneness with the Absolute. [18:53]

Jnaneshwar Maharaj comments on this:

> The seeker destroys anger, the greatest of vices, anger which becomes more useless the more it is fostered.
>
> As he removes all trace of desire, he eradicates anger along with it.
>
> When the roots are cut, the branches of a tree wither; similarly, when desire dies, anger dies with it.
>
> So when the enemy called desire is killed in this battle, anger suffers the same fate.

After the first talk on anger, somebody asked, "I have a desire for knowledge. Is that bad, too? Am I supposed to get rid of it?" If you have a desire for knowledge, this is *sattva guna*. If you put it to use and achieve the highest *without* getting tangled in the three qualities, you will have an experience of the Truth. On the other hand, if you become filled with the pride of learning, you are stuck in *sattva guna*. When you put that into action, it is *rajoguna*. When you rest on your laurels and get lazy, staring idly into space, as if deep in thought, *tamoguna* comes into play. There you are, once again, completely enmeshed in the three qualities.

We are on the spiritual path. We want to attain the highest, we want to know the Truth. So don't try to justify or fool yourself by saying this particular desire is okay, that desire is not okay, this desire is fine, that one is not. Look at the root of every desire. Examine it. Don't just use it as an opportunity for small talk or to show off your knowledge of the *Bhagavad Gītā*. Examine it honestly. If you want to talk to somebody, talk in such a way that your statement provokes contemplation instead of an argument or a challenge or a useless debate. Let this very conversation be the one that takes you to the Truth.

To understand the lesson that Lord Krishna is teaching Arjuna, you have to understand why the great war of the *Mahābhārata* was fought. Two sides of the same family, the Pandavas and the Kauravas, had a desire to rule the land. This desire, when it was frustrated, led to anger and ultimately to war. When at first Arjuna was ready to fight, it was with these motives: desire, wanting to rule, wanting to conquer—and anger, the urge to destroy his so-called enemies.

Arjuna was a warrior and a veteran of numerous battles. He knew the taste of self-righteous anger and the desire to fight for what he believed in. He had triumphed over all manner of men and demons in this way. So he believed that these feelings were indispensable to him. He associated the rush of their fire in his blood with victory. But on that morning, as the war was about to begin, something was different.

Arjuna looked around him on the battlefield, and there, in the bright light of morning, he saw all his cousins, his uncles, his teachers and his elders, the playmates and rivals of his childhood, his kinsmen. Instead of facing an army of enemies, he found himself looking into the eyes of his friends — the glorious Bhishma, the man of wisdom, and the mighty Karna, and Ashvatthama, and Kuntibhoja; Drona, the teacher he idolized; and his cousins, his own flesh and blood. Each face pierced his heart. In that moment, Arjuna lost his whole sense of purpose, and all his courage drained away. Their faces were a mirror, and what he saw in it disarmed him. He saw his own anger and desire, clearly reflected and standing before him.

Until then, Arjuna's conscience had been somewhat opaque. So everything he did seemed fine to him. But now the mist was gone. His conscience sparkled, clear as crystal, and it began to ask him questions about what he was doing. It prompted him to look at his motives and question the passions surging through his body.

This was such a new experience for Arjuna, the questions were so unfamiliar, the answers so startling that his instinctive reaction was to drop his weapons and refuse to fight. "Why fight?" he said. That was the only way he saw to renounce his desire and his anger. Truly speaking, he did not know how to fight without them. Desire and anger had always been the source of his energy, his great strength. His adrenal glands only worked in *rajoguna*, personal glory, personal gain, pure and impure impulses all tangled up in each other, a commotion of motives and reactions.

For this reason, Lord Krishna compassionately stopped Arjuna and gave him the teachings contained in the *Bhagavad Gītā*. Arjuna's motives for fighting were purified and he could take the field to preserve dharma. Grounded in the knowledge of the Self and the wisdom of right action, he was ready to act out of *sattva guna*, pure motives, without a trace of selfishness. So, the battle would be fought with justice, and the outcome was bound to be righteous, for dharma always wins.

This is the way it has always been, from Guru to disciple, Guru to disciple, throughout history. This is the way the teachings have been handed down. Life is a battlefield. One constantly has to fight to meet the challenges of life. However, to fight for supreme Truth, a person must empty himself of all the wrong intentions and become pure, utterly pure, within. To attain liberation, one must fight on this battlefield of life against one's own inner enemies. At the same time, one must preserve dharma.

With the power of dharma comes the conviction "This is the only thing to do." As long as you are wondering, "Is this right or is that right? . . . Is this wrong? Or is it right? . . . What should I do? . . . It's not wrong, is it? . . . Is this all right?" as long as you find yourself in this sort of dilemma, chances are, your motives are less than dharmic. If you are acting out of this kind of idea of right and wrong, you are completely enmeshed with the three gunas, the qualities. You are not experiencing the Self at all. When you act out of the experience of dharma and the Self, nothing can deflect you, nothing can dissuade you, and nothing can defeat you. When a seeker has won his freedom from desire and anger, then all the other virtues begin to shine in great splendor.

This is why you come to the ashram. It is a wonderful place to do sadhana. Whatever stage of spiritual development you have reached, that is fine. You must not compare yourself or the degree of sadhana you are doing with others. You should not lose time wondering how you seem in other people's eyes. Instead you should always wonder, how does God see you? How do you want to be seen in God's eyes? The universe, no matter how much you try to do, is not in your hands. Nevertheless, God has given you the freedom to work on your own universe and also to experience the fruits of your true and good actions.

With great respect and great love, I welcome you all with all my heart.

August 1, 1993

CHAPTER SEVEN

Compassion

Dayā

WITH GREAT RESPECT, WITH GREAT LOVE, I welcome you all with all my heart.

You may do many of your spiritual practices in the company of other people, but sadhana is a process that takes place within you. When you chant, if your heart is completely open, waves of nectar wash over you. Even if your heart is not completely open, somehow the nectar deep inside you seeps through anyway. During meditation, if your mind happens to wander, no one else is responsible. You can't really go around complaining about it. You have to look within. When the obstacle is external, however, you can actually complain. You can turn your attention outside and let yourself go. Of course, you can also choose to make use of the obstacle; you can see it as an opportunity to cultivate one of the virtues named in the *Bhagavad Gītā.*

We have been looking at these virtues very carefully, one by one; and many people have shared their experiences of the process of cultivating them. Some say it is very difficult. Still, they say, once they overcame whatever obstacle they were confronted with, they experienced the beauty of these virtues. Then they tried to practice holding the virtue for a longer and longer period of time, so that they could actually taste it and put it into action.

Many people have talked about overcoming the sensation of anger, in particular. Some say they have made an effort to understand how and why they become angry. They have retraced this emotion all the way to its source, and there, instead of anger, they have discovered their own true Self. So there is that great Self. Even though you do sadhana in the name of overcoming negativities and the inner enemies, what you experience finally is your own great Self. Underneath everything, there is Consciousness.

Tonight we will be discussing *dayā*, the magnificent virtue of compassion. The root of the English word *compassion* is twofold: *com*, meaning together in Latin; and *pati*, meaning to suffer. Compassion is defined as the spiritual consciousness of another person's pain, and a feeling of unselfish tenderness directed toward him.

Baba Muktananda was the epitome of this kind of compassion. He once said, "We are always saying that man is a high, sublime, and noble being. The light of God shines in man. His heart is filled with God's compassion and love. But he doesn't know it. When you go to sleep, you get some rest. But when you meditate and reach that place in the heart, you find complete and total peace, total rest, in God. The divine flame of God is blazing in everyone, and everyone should make an effort to see it."

You must allow yourself to be arrested by God's love and compassion. The modern world has labored very hard for efficiency, so that everyone might enjoy immediate results and quick profits. As Baba sometimes said, everybody wants shortcuts. The modern world has also put forth such enormous effort to make people independent and self-sufficient. It has gone to incredible lengths to make our lives convenient in every way. If you wanted to fill a house with all the gadgets and time-savers in existence, it would have to be a mansion with many, many, many floors. Perhaps it would reach all the way to heaven. But what has all this done to the human psyche?

Every living thing is selfish by nature. Every human being is also selfish to some degree. You might say selfishness is second nature to the human race. So, by freeing a person's time and energy from all constraints, from everything and everybody else, hasn't the modern world also cut a person off from his own innate capacity for compassion? Compassion, a virtue which is so simple and yet so far-reaching in its effects.

When you don't know how compassion really feels, you may not understand why you should aspire to it. Compassion is the divine impulse that stirs within you when you come across someone's ignorance or pain. And I don't just mean someone who is ailing physically. Think about the compassion of a great being. Baba Muktananda's compassion was so vast and powerful that when you came into his presence, you would enter your own heart.

Compassion such as this is so stirring that it is said to make even rocks weep with love. It is not just a feeling that arises and subsides from time to time. When you reach the goal, as Baba had, you become the embodiment of compassion. So wherever you go, everybody knows they will receive help. As they feel your presence, they also feel security, great safety. It isn't that you will be performing one or two great feats. Just your presence is enough, because you carry the tenderness of the heart, the loving heart.

This supreme compassion exists in everyone. Therefore, all the great beings say, come into the realm of your heart. Bathe in the light of your own heart. Drink the nectar of compassion from the wellspring of your own heart. Don't look for compassion anywhere else, from anyone else. It is inside you. You are the owner of this great virtue.

The practice of compassion is so potent that one tiny service has the power to purify your thoughts and burn your selfishness to a crisp. As you make the effort to let compassion be your guide, instead of your self-centered judgment of a situation or a person, then you find yourself being rocked in the cradle of your own divine heart. Your heart will never have walls again. Compassion is such a great virtue that it melts the walls around the heart.

Have you ever come across people who seem at first to have a great sense of humor? Whatever they say is so funny, you laugh and you laugh and you laugh. However, there's no joy in it, not really. At first, you think it's your fault. Eventually, you realize their humor is not true, somehow. It's not the delight of the Self. It's only sarcasm; or worse, all the laughter is at someone else's expense. It's nervous laughter, with an edge of discomfort. In this kind of humor, there is no compassion. No one is uplifted. People like this, who systematically make fun of others, are also very uncomfortable with their own lives and, if the truth be told, with their own view of reality. The only way they know to make themselves comfortable is by cracking jokes about the flaws in other people. They have no compassion.

Compassion is a very delicate trait. Many people feel genuinely sorry and upset when they see a beggar or a mangy dog, or an accident of any kind. But there is a great difference between pity and compassion. When you feel pity, you put yourself in the other person's place. You think, if you had an accident, if you were sick, you'd want someone to help you. Bearing that in mind, you go and help another. That is pity. Or perhaps you help with the attitude that someday that person will help you in return, or because it is gratifying to you personally. You are really focusing on yourself, instead of the one in pain.

In cases like these, the mind does not expand into a greater awareness, it does not become pure, and it does not experience joy. In true compassion, your thoughts become pure and your heart experiences its integrity, its dignity, its wholesomeness. You feel completely renewed. The boon, the blessing, of compassion is much greater than the pale imitations produced by pity. In compassion, the heart literally moves with love, and the one who inspires it receives love, and healing too. Compassion takes on another person's misery without any strings attached and gives the one who is suffering complete consolation. You look at him with love in your eyes, you experience his suffering, and immediately that person is fine, really fine.

Have you ever experienced compassion, even if it is just a little bit, a mist of compassion? Take a moment and think about it. Have you ever felt compassion, and if you have, have you ever allowed it to grow? Have you ever let the mist of compassion become the ocean of compassion? Have you ever asked for grace so that your compassion may increase?

What do you really feel when someone is miserable? Do you merely say, "Oh, I feel bad for you. I wish that hadn't happened to you," or do you extend a helping hand? And if you do try to help, what, if anything, do you expect in exchange?

In the Middle Ages, when kings were many and there were fortresses on the tops of many mountains, two kings in neighboring realms fell into a quarrel. Soon their armies were battling it out on the fields and valleys between their castles. Late one afternoon, one of the kings was captured by the opposing army. That night, they threw this king down an empty well, so there was no chance of his escaping. They set up camp and triumphantly began to celebrate the night away. Now, as the night passed, it so happened that a local man, who considered himself to be quite a scholar, was passing that way and he heard a voice crying out, "Help! Help me!"

The fellow found the well and peered inside it. "Who are you?" he said. "And what are you doing down there?"

"I'm the king," whispered the king. "Please save me! Please, please, get me out of here."

Being a bit of a scholar, it didn't take the fellow long to figure out what was going on. He found a rope and helped the king out of the well. It all happened very quickly and quietly, and soon they were walking away from the enemy camp. But as soon as the monarch was beside him, shoulder to shoulder, the fellow seemed overwhelmed.

"I can't believe it!" he said. "I saved you. I saved the king! Me! Isn't it wonderful?"

The king was just as happy. "Oh yes," he said. "O my good fellow, thank you so much. With all my heart, I want to thank God for sending you this way. Thank you, thank you."

And they began to walk again. But after a few steps, the man stopped the king, saying, "Pinch me! Is this really real? Pinch me!" And the king did, and then the man said, "This is the greatest day of my life. O King! Do you realize? I saved you. *I* saved *you.* Wait until my neighbors hear about this! And the court! I suppose you'll tell everybody in court. I mean, in their eyes, I'm a hero."

And the king agreed. He pledged to tell everyone what happened and offered a series of very handsome rewards. He said it would be his pleasure, he was grateful, he would never forget what had happened. But now, if the man didn't mind, they had better be quiet for they were still within range of the enemy. "They are right over there," he said. "Celebrating my capture. If we're not careful, they might hear us. So let's be silent and get back to court quickly."

And the man agreed. Then, two seconds later, he forgot. "I'm so excited," he said. "You'll be introducing me to so many people and telling them I saved you. It's going to be, it's going to be *in*-credible."

The king stopped walking. Very sternly, he looked at the local man and then he looked up at the heavens. And then the king let out a scream. "The king is escaping!" he shouted. "The king is escaping! Catch him! Catch him!"

The enemy guards came running, and of course, they found the king. Immediately, they put him back in chains, along with the man who was standing beside him, shaking in his boots. As they were escorting the king back to the well, one of the soldiers spoke. "Your Majesty, you could have escaped very easily. You were halfway gone. Why did you let yourself be captured again?"

And the king replied, "I would rather be here in chains than spend the rest of my life in the prison of this man's good deed."

It is never easy to cultivate virtues. You have to go through a painful process, it is true. When it comes to helping others, you have to be especially careful. You have to reflect on your motives and your interests. Are you doing something because it is gratifying to you, or because there is a reward of some kind? Or are you doing it because you really want to help? You have to do a great deal of self-inquiry to be able to tell; you have to contemplate every ripple of thought that goes through your mind. When you display compassion, the other person can often sense your motives much more pointedly than you can.

In the *Bhagavad Gītā,* Lord Krishna urges Arjuna to cultivate these various virtues so that Arjuna will be able to fight in a dharmic war. Compassion is a noble virtue. To be compassionate, you must learn to think well of yourself and others. Therefore a bleeding heart, which sees other people as helpless, is not a sign of compassion.

According to Buddhism, compassion uproots pain and suffering. When the compassion you feel for someone is genuine, you experience the light of dharma, of righteousness, of right action, shining inside you. So this virtue called *dayā*, compassion, is filled with great wisdom. Another word for compassion is *karūna*, the mercy of God. Every day after the text of the *Guru Gītā*, we chant *Āratī Karūn*. In this prayer we appeal to God and the Guru to have compassion for us and remove all our suffering and pain.

Have you ever immersed yourself in the ocean of compassion? Compassion is a divine quality. Out of compassion, we have been given existence. Out of our selfishness, we have mutilated it. How can you come to any understanding of compassion when you are still clinging to the hems of selfishness? Isn't compassion the cry of the heart, the tears of the soul?

A modern author once said, "Few men really want justice; what all mankind prays for is mercy."

Out of compassion, a tree grows. Out of compassion, a river flows to the sea. Out of compassion, the tiger lets you go. Out of compassion, your mind becomes still. Out of compassion, you release your grip on attachment.

How can this supreme compassion ever be taught? It can only be lived out. It is out of compassion that the Master draws a disciple to his heart. How can compassion such as this ever be confined, like beads to a string, when its very nature is *svātantrya*, absolute freedom? How can you contain the ocean in a thimble? This is why, to contain the great ocean of Consciousness, your heart has to expand.

Kashmir Shaivism says, "This Consciousness is vibrating light. It is Absolute Reality, beyond all spatial and temporal distinctions. This Consciousness, which is the essence of the cosmos, is called the heart of God."

Isn't it our own selfishness which puts drops of lemon juice in milk and then says, "Oh, this milk has gone sour!" Isn't it our selfishness which throws black tar in someone's face and then says, "That person has such a tarnished reputation!" Isn't it selfishness that makes us shamelessly accuse God of our own shortcomings?

How can grain last in the granary if thousands of mice are feeding on it daily? How can plants survive if bugs are eating away at them? Don't you know selfishness erodes everything good that you have? Isn't it time you let the fragrance of compassion permeate your being?

Watch your own thoughts. You can do this in complete freedom. Scientists have not yet come up with a gadget to put against your head and find out what you are thinking. The power of all the words and images you create in your mind, your *mātrikā shakti,* is entirely your own possession. Only you hold the key to your thoughts. Nobody can steal them from you. Only you can spill them out, in words or in actions. And your thoughts mold your life. Your happiness and your unhappiness, your good fortune and your misfortune, your patience and your impatience, all this depends on your own thoughts and feelings. You are in charge. You have the authority to keep your thoughts in check or let them run wild. When you have a negative thought, you can look at it and see if you can change its pattern. When you have a bad feeling toward somebody and an impulse to act on it, you have a choice. You can pause and see if that is really what you want to do. You are in charge.

You know, lots of people say they have problems with authority. They never want to comply with it; they only want to question it. So maybe there is a problem after all—since you have full authority over yourself. Maybe your problem is with yourself.

People try many different paths to rid themselves of suffering and misery. They seek to know the Self. However, for this, what really matters is humility, and humility only appears when selfishness is cut away. Selfishness is the enemy of all the magnificent virtues. It blinds you to their value and tricks you into settling for lesser things.

Selfishness grows out of doership. It wants to take the credit for everything and it fears humiliation. In the business world, people experience this sort of thing all the time. In a partnership, there is very often one partner who continually tries to take credit for everything and cheat the other partner out of his share. Yet this very selfishness, this sense of doership, doesn't want to be discovered. Only the great Self wants to be found out. All these inner forms of pettiness try to avoid discovery, because it is in the dark that they grow, like mushrooms.

Selfishness is a barrier that keeps greater light from streaming in. When you pray to your chosen deity with total humility, you elicit that deity's compassion. During your prayer, you may appear to be pleading and begging, baring your soul. It may look like you are putting yourself down, but actually you are just revealing all that you have done and not done. You are openly accepting your attachment to your various shortcomings and admitting it to yourself before the form of God you worship, before the Absolute, the great authority, the supreme Witness.

In his prayer to the Goddess, the great spiritual Master Shankaracharya accepts all his faults and lays them at Her feet. At the time he wrote this hymn, Shankaracharya had already written commentaries on many of the scriptures; he had expounded Vedanta and carried it to the four corners of India; he had founded monastic orders and erected monasteries; and yet, when he prayed, it was with utter humility. Baba always said, no matter how great you become, always remain a disciple. This is Baba's formula for greatness, so that your heart never becomes stiff and brittle with false pride. In the hymn he composed to the Divine Mother for forgiveness, Shankaracharya prayed:

I know, alas, no hymn, no mantra,
Neither prayer nor meditation,
Nor even how to praise You.
The proper ritual of worship,
How to place the hands and make supplication, I know not.
But Mother, this at least I know:
Whoever turns to You for refuge
Reaches the end of all his misery.

Bewildered by the rules of conduct,
By the injunctions of the scriptures,
I have abandoned, one by one,
The shining gods; and now my life
Is more than halfway gone.

Mother, should You withhold Your mercy,
Where can I look for shelter,
Weak and helpless as I am?

Mother, I have not worshiped You with proper rituals,
Or the prescribed ingredients of sacrifice.
Many are my sins!
Days and nights I have wasted
In idle talk, forgetting You.
O Divine Mother, if You can show
The slightest mercy to one so frail,
It will befit Your majesty.

O Durga, goddess of Mercy's ocean,
Grief-stricken, I implore you.
Do not believe me insincere.
A child who is seized with thirst and hunger
Thinks of his mother constantly.

Only out of humility can one truly pray. When you offer your feelings of insignificance and worthlessness to your chosen deity, to your God or your Guru, your tears wash all this away. Unfailingly, when you give your heart to God, there is grace, there is light. Not only do you have the experience of God's compassion and God's light but you also realize that is what you are and, from the beginning, always have been. Your nature is light.

Compassion transcends the physical plane. Selfishness, on the other hand, gets stuck at the physical level. When you look at someone in frustration and say, "You're so selfish," or even think such a thing, it means that you yourself have not gone beyond the barrier of appearances. What do you know about their life? How can you know what they have gone through? Selfishness stops at the physical plane. Unless you pass through that barrier, you cannot experience compassion, let alone express it.

Baba Muktananda has walked the grounds of the South Fallsburg ashram. He has gone to almost every corner of this place. You must allow yourself to experience his subtle presence. His compassion and his blessings permeate the atmosphere. He is here.

Recently, I got a letter from one of the people here. She actually didn't want to be in South Fallsburg. She wanted to go to the ashram in Ganeshpuri. Baba spent so many years there, she thought that is where she would be able to experience his presence. Still, because her husband wanted to spend time here in South Fallsburg, she agreed to come. Recently, she said, she and her husband were sitting in their room silently and all of a sudden they inhaled a fragrance they recognized. It was one of the scented oils that Baba used —either *heena* or *khus.* He used to put it on the peacock feathers that he held when he gave darshan, or when he gave shaktipat. They both experienced this incredible fragrance simultaneously, in silence. And then, later, one said, "I felt Baba. I could sense his presence and his fragrance." And the other said, "Me, too." And they were filled with great joy, great delight. In her letter, she said, "I know Baba is here, too, and I am so happy to be in South Fallsburg."

You can allow yourself to experience the great Shakti, the great energy that Siddhas carry, the great power that Baba Muktananda has. Just remember that selfishness keeps you stuck on the physical plane, and compassion allows you to pierce that level of reality and experience the light of the Self.

Baba Muktananda said, "The very nature of the Self, the great Self, is love, and because its nature is love, compassion flows from it. Compassion does not imply a pose to cheat people. It does not imply soft words or soft gestures just to throw dust into another's eyes. Compassion is the source from which grace flows and from which shaktipat is given."

This great virtue exists in everybody, but we have lost touch with it. We must give ourselves time, we must give ourselves a chance to experience it. The sensation is so profound. When you are filled with compassion, you will notice that every cell in your body tingles and you can see Consciousness shimmering everywhere.

This morning, a father was recounting the experience of his son who had been here a couple of weeks ago. When the teenager came home he was so completely changed, his father couldn't believe it. The boy said, "Father, I saw God in every leaf in the ashram." He was so moved. In fact, I remember the time this young man came for darshan after the Teen Intensive and said to me, "Gurumayi, will you forgive me for being so mean to my parents all these years, for not understanding their love? I truly want to be forgiven. I really do."

I asked him to go and speak to someone in particular. This person advised him to call his parents right away and let them know what he was feeling. That is exactly what he did. He called them on the phone and said, "I have asked for forgiveness. I have gone to Gurumayi," and he repeated the whole thing.

His parents were completely touched. When the father came, later this summer, he couldn't stop talking about his son the whole time. Whenever I saw him, he would tell me the story all over again. "My son, my son, I saw the tears of transformation in his eyes. I heard his voice change. My son saw God in every leaf."

I kept nodding. "Yes, yes." It was truly beautiful. When you hear somebody speaking of an experience of transformation, it moves you. Every time you think you have heard it enough, it touches another part of your being. You realize "Oh, there is something more . . ." in the way the person says it, in the way that it affects you. Compassion. When you share a feeling of compassion, you are able to see God in each other.

With great respect and great love, I welcome you all with all my heart.

August 14, 1993

CHAPTER EIGHT

HUMILITY

Prahva

WITH GREAT RESPECT AND GREAT LOVE, I welcome you all with all my heart.

There is a great philosophical text called the *Viveka Chūdāmani*, "The Crest Jewel of Discrimination." It was written by the sage Shankaracharya in the eighth century and it is a model of the clarity and beauty of an enlightened mind. In one of its verses, Shankaracharya speaks about virtue, specifically about the virtues of a true seeker. Shankaracharya says,

> *tam-ārādhya gurum̧ bhaktyā prahva-praśhraya-sevanaiḥ /*
> *prasannam̧ tam-anuprāpya pṛicchej-jñātavyam-ātmanaḥ //*

> Let the seeker approach the Master with reverent devotion. Then, when he has pleased him by his humility, respect, and service, let him ask whatever may be known about the *ātman*, the supreme Self. [34]

Humility is a very delicate quality. It is said that the moment you think you have humility, you have lost it. Since that is the case, how can it even be described? You cannot sneak up on humility. It is the product of a very high level of awareness and will always see you coming. However, perhaps a few examples will help. A

Christian saint once said, "Humility is to the virtues what the chain is to the rosary. Remove the chain and all the beads escape. Take away humility, and all other virtues disappear."

Have you ever heard of the legendary Arab king named Hatim Tai? Sa'di, the great Sufi mystic and poet, tells a beautiful story about him. Hatim was deaf, you know, or so people thought for many years. But early one morning, when the council chambers were nearly deserted, a soft buzzing, almost a hum, began in a corner of the room. And Hatim Tai got up and walked over to it.

He found a fly struggling in a spider's web. The strands of the web glistened like spun sugar in the morning sun. Had the fly mistaken them for candy? Did he think the spider, crouching motionless in a high corner of the web, was a chunk of dark sugar?

Hatim spoke to the fly, "O you who are shackled by desire, hold still! Now you know that you don't find sweet things everywhere you look. In some corners, traps and bonds await you!" In another moment, the spider darted forward and the buzzing stopped. Hatim Tai turned away with a sad smile.

There were only a few other people in the room that morning. One of them, a simple soldier spoke up. "Sire," he said, marveling. "How did you know about the fly? I could hardly hear it all the way over here. O man upon the way of God, forgive me! But none should call you deaf. You hear better than I do."

"You're a clever fellow," said Hatim Tai. "Believe me, it is far better to be thought deaf than to have to listen to empty praise. Shall I tell you how my deafness began? It started the day that I realized I was surrounded by people who coated all my faults with compliments. I was caught in a web of flattery and praise; and to be honest, both my character and my judgment were deteriorating. So I decided to let people think I couldn't hear them anymore and, little by little, they stopped trying to influence me that way.

"When those who sit with me in these chambers think I can't hear, they are not afraid to say what's wrong with me. And if I am not always pleased by what they say, then I try to change the behavior that provoked their words. Deafness, on the whole, has served me very well. It has saved me all these years from the vices that come with vanity. You might try it some day, young man. Do not let yourself be pulled over the edge of a bottomless well by ropes of praise. Be deaf, like Hatim, and listen to your faults."

Humility is the way to God. All the other virtues flock to it. They cannot resist it. Baba Muktananda was a great being, so great in fact that the virtues went looking for him. They wanted to be in his company. When you make your heart very clean, it is said, the virtues come to dwell in your being. Speaking about humility once, Baba said, "In your worldly life, people may be impressed by your family or by other external factors. But, as far as God is concerned, He pays absolutely no attention to your body, to its beauty or to your facial features. He doesn't pay any attention to your sense organs. He only values the feelings in your heart. An Upanishadic seer said that one who considers the body to be his Self is committing a sin equivalent to the slaughter of a million cows.

"In the divine realm, in the realm of meditation, your family consciousness is of no use, your vows are of no use, your status is of no use, the power that you wield is of no use. There, only complete humility, complete surrender and devotion matter. Only they will take you deeper into meditation."

When you walk the path of humility, your destination is God. Baba continued, "Remember that consciousness of the body, pride in the body, attachment to the body will certainly bring about your downfall one day or another."

How do you approach a spiritual Master? A deity? A child? Nature itself? With humility. If you want to receive their love, their grace, their blessings, the scriptures say, you must approach with a humble heart.

It is true you cannot talk about humility. You cannot put humility on display and show it off. It is something that takes birth in the heart. When it does, your heart becomes vulnerable and very tender. This only means you have become stronger. Perhaps that is why a great author once said, "I don't want any philosophy which doesn't carry the tears of the heart." A heart made vulnerable by humility gains the courage of God. It becomes solid. It loses its whimsical emotions and becomes established in the Truth, which is God's love.

Every religious tradition speaks about humility with reverence, and every mystical path seems to have many stories to tell about it. This is not only because humility is so difficult to define but also because this virtue—indispensable and yet invisible, incredibly tender and yet able to bear any weight—is so dear to the heart of a mystic. In the Hasidic tradition of Judaism, they tell a beautiful story about humility. It goes like this:

Once, in a small village in Eastern Europe, there lived a rich man who never gave alms to the poor or to any charity of any kind. People in those parts never called him by his name. He was known to them all as The Miser. If a beggar ever came to this rich man's door, the miser always asked him where he was from. "You can't be from anywhere around here," he would say. "Everyone in this village knows better than to ask me for money!"

In the same village, there lived a poor shoemaker. He was an extremely generous man. No one in need was ever turned away from his door. He gave to every beggar he saw and to every good cause. Whenever calamity struck a family, in the form of an illness or an accident, the shoemaker was always ready to help. "Just a little something," he would say, "to tide you over."

One day the miser died. Everyone has to die sooner or later. Today someone goes. Tomorrow, it's someone else. One day it's me, the next day it's you. We all have to empty this world out so that other souls can be born on the planet. When the miser died, he was not mourned. No one followed his coffin to its final resting place. No one prayed on his behalf. In fact, the village elders decided to bury him at the far end of the cemetery, since he had cared so little for other people or their welfare.

As the days passed, the rabbi of that village began to hear disturbing news about the shoemaker. "He no longer seems to care about people," it was said. "He won't give a penny to anyone. He refuses every charity and every beggar who comes to his door, no matter how worthy or hungry they are."

"Has anyone asked the shoemaker about this?" the rabbi inquired.

"Yes," one man replied. "He says he needs all his money for himself."

It was very odd. The rabbi decided to call on the shoemaker and ask him for an explanation. "Is there something wrong? What has happened to change your heart?"

The shoemaker hesitated. Then, after a long pause, he began to speak. "Many years ago, the man you called the miser came to me with a huge sum of money. He asked me to give it away in charity. He made me promise never to reveal his name or our arrangement as long as he lived. And since he paid me a small salary for the service, I agreed. Once every month, he visited me late at night and handed me money to give away. And if I had not distributed every cent by the next time he came, he would become very annoyed. I became known as a great benefactor, even though I never spent a penny of my own money. Frankly, I'm surprised nobody ever asked me about it before. How could a shoemaker possibly give away as much money as I have all these years?"

The rabbi called all the villagers together and told them the story. "The miser lived by the scriptures, keeping his charity a secret," the rabbi said. "He asked for nothing in return. He wanted nothing for himself. This is the sign of a humble heart." The whole village walked to the cemetery that day and prayed beside the rough, untended grave. After the prayers for the dead had been recited, the rabbi spoke in a trembling voice, "When I die, I ask only one thing of you. Please bury me here, next to the humble man known as the miser."

One of the signs of humility is this: neither seeking nor expecting credit for your actions. Most people perform one-fourth of a good deed and they want the whole world to know about it. But who ever thinks of contemplating the fundamental question, "Where did I come from?" Not in the philosophical sense that can be answered "I am born of Brahman, I live in Brahman and finally I will merge into Brahman, the Absolute Reality." It is a matter of looking into a much simpler question than that. "What are my motivations? How have I kept the state of my heart?"

Everyone always prefers to look at other people instead. They would rather ask, "How are *they* treating me? How are *they* affecting my life, and my state? Why won't they say the things that make me happy; why won't they do, why won't they give me what I want?" It is very difficult for someone to turn his attention away from others, to look honestly into his own heart and ask the same crucial questions, "What kind of life am I creating for another person? What kind of *world* am I creating?"

Humility. This is another one of the signs of its presence — taking responsibility for your own world, putting yourself aside and thinking well of others, contemplating your actions with the sincere wish to improve. At first glance, it may seem that these things go against the grain of instinct. If one person uses an abusive term, for instance, the immediate impulse is to respond with an even more abusive one. But do you ever stop to think "What have I done to create this exchange? To what extent am I responsible?"

These questions stop you in your tracks. They force you to contemplate.

How must you approach a spiritual Master? A child? A tree? A deity? A king? A noble soul? You must approach them with humility if you want to receive their grace. It is not enough to perform one or two wonderful deeds and expect the rest of your life to be filled with gold and diamonds and rubies, with fame and reputation. If you do, you will be sorely disappointed.

Humility is a rare attainment. Even making the effort is a labor of love. Sometimes you may feel your heart is bleeding. At other times, you may feel that your heart has gone so dry, you experience nothing. At other moments, you feel your heart soaring, soaring in bliss. Humility has all these different flavors. Your heart may go through many different moods and experiences but you do not stop there. You examine your thoughts, your speech, your actions. Every time you perform a good and true action, you pause and ask, "What is my state? Am I giving my happiness to this work, or am I filling it with my anger?"

If you have the fortitude to examine yourself honestly in this way, humility is not far off. As all the great ones have said, this virtue is a part of your own nature. It cannot be bought. It must be uncovered as a labor of love. Through self-examination, you attain it from within.

The great poet-saint Jnaneshwar Maharaj described the essence of humility in chapter thirteen of his commentary on the *Bhagavad Gītā*:

> Such a person doesn't strive for success in any worldly matter and feels any honor to be a burden.
>
> If people praise his qualities, if they show him respect, or if they recognize his greatness,
>
> He feels embarrassed, like a deer trapped by a hunter, or a swimmer caught in a whirlpool.
>
> He doesn't want others to see any sign of his worthiness, or to hear any word of his fame. He prefers that other people not remember him as having any special qualities.
>
> Such a person has no wish to receive respect or honor. He prefers death to receiving a salutation.
>
> He conceals his knowledge, makes no use of his high attainments, and prefers to be considered mad.
>
> He is happy to be ignored and doesn't want his own relatives to notice him. This is the way he likes to live.
>
> He behaves in such a way that people will consider him lowly. Humility is like a jewel to him.
>
> He desires that people should never know whether he walks by himself or whether he is propelled by the wind.
>
> He prefers that his existence should be hidden and his name unknown, so that no creature will fear him.
>
> He is content with the company of the wind, takes pleasure in conversing with the sky, and loves trees as his own life.
>
> A person in whom these characteristics are found is the intimate companion of knowledge.

This is the highest glory of humility. It cannot be attained in the wink of an eye. It is the work of lifetimes. Nevertheless, we can take one step at a time. The first step is to stop thinking of it as something inaccessible or out of reach. The second step is to give it a try. For example, when you are sitting in the dining hall and you find yourself alone at a table, you ought to be able to enjoy it, instead of thinking "No one likes me," or looking at someone else who—

unlike you — has lots and lots of friends. Instead of worrying about your destiny or letting your mind wander, instead of finding fault with yourself and others, you might actually watch your own breath. You might give yourself a chance to feel what is arising in your heart.

You are the temple of God. Ask yourself: what is your heart trying to tell you? Ask yourself: what sound is this, reverberating in the vast silence of your being? Where does it come from? What is it made of? Pay attention to the virtues that exist within you. That is how you attain grace, not by throwing tantrums, or arguing with the scriptures, not by debating with the Guru. You can draw all that knowledge and all that grace through the power of humility alone.

The teachings of the Siddhas, the great Masters, are being delivered constantly in the words of the people around you and in the actions of strangers. Try to develop this understanding: there is a great lesson to be learned; God is teaching you humility.

In the end, all that really matters is the state of your heart. However you have kept yourself, that is what finally goes with you. That is the fruit of your life in this world.

A great devotee of the Lord once expressed his humility through this prayer:

> O Lord, I have come to Your feet to try and please You and
> win Your heart.
> My speech is crude, without the least bit of sweetness,
> Yet I have come to make You hear my plea.
>
> O Lord, I am not worthy to receive the nectar that flows
> at Your feet,
> Nor do I have anything in which to hold it.
> Still the cups of my eyes have come to beg for something
> from You.
> What gifts do I have to offer at Your feet?
> I am only a beggar, while You are the giver.
> So I have come to tell You about our relationship.
>
> I don't really know what service means,
> Yet look at my courage:

Today I have come before you, weeping,
To offer you the garland of my tears.

When you can give your heart to God freely, you receive everything. When you come before the Lord, you must come with no concepts and no illusions. You must come with humility. That is when you experience the gift of grace. A heart filled with humility becomes a pool of nectar. You experience your own tears as the nectar of love. A heart this tender is still so strong that it can soar in the space of Consciousness. Always remember, it is a sign of humility to let go of the limitations that keep you from knowing the natural wonder of your own heart.

This was Baba Muktananda's message to the world:

Meditate on your own Self,
Worship your own Self,
God dwells within you as you.

With great respect and great love, I welcome you all with all my heart.

December 26, 1993

CHAPTER NINE

Respect

Praśhraya

WITH GREAT RESPECT AND GREAT LOVE, I welcome you all with all my heart.

Time has gone by so quickly. And yet, for some people it has already been such a long, long year. For some people, the time has been filled with birthdays, celebrations, and many wonderful things. For other people, it has been a time of tragedy and tribulation. Will they approach the end of the year in the same way? With so many resolutions still on their list — not answered, not fulfilled, just sitting there, like dead weight, making the notebooks heavier and heavier? Just by passing, time increases their burden.

However, time can also be very kind. If you treat time with respect, then time is your friend. There is a saying, "The great rule of moral conduct is, next to God, to respect time." If you have respected time, then it really doesn't matter whether it goes by quickly or draws itself out to eternity. If you have made friends with time, it doesn't matter how young or old you look, either. Physical age is irrelevant. If you have been good to time, everything is fine.

People are always talking about "good times" and "bad times." Haven't you noticed? They talk about "wonderful times" and "agonizing times," "pleasant times" and "painful times." Is time the problem? Is it really? Time, which is God itself, time, which can be measured and yet is beyond space, time, which is formless. How can time be good or bad? It is a second. It is an hour. It is a day. It is night.

Who is it that colors time all these different ways? Who is painting this particular moment, right now, with different images and visions? Could it be you?

When you say, for instance, "I was so happy, I had such a good time when Swamiji was the master of ceremonies at the evening program," what does that mean? Now, the swamis are the same every day, basically. So it was not that this particular swami created an exceptionally happy time for you. It was that you listened to him with a happy heart. Therefore, what he said entered your heart and you experienced joy. Let's take another example. Sometimes you say, "That boy Michael gives me such a hard time every day." But is your hard time really his doing? True, it is his nature to say bad things. He is always going to say something to upset you. You can count on it. Michael has mastered the art of agitating people. The question is, knowing this, why do you expose your heart in a way that allows him to fill you with negativities? Who is really responsible?

As long as we nourish a tendency to blame others for the way we fill our time, our good times will always be brief. As long as we do not make friends with time, time will always seem to deal with us unkindly. How we treat time, therefore, is very significant. Soon one season will come to an end. But another is beginning. So there is still time. You can take this time and make it yours, make it valuable, make it divine, and live in bliss.

For the last several months, we have been discussing the magnificent virtues described by Lord Krishna to his disciple Arjuna in the *Bhagavad Gītā*. Yesterday we began to enlarge our discussion to include three virtues that are mentioned by the great sage Shankaracharya in his text, *Viveka Chūdāmani*, "The Crest Jewel of Discrimination." In this particular verse, Shankaracharya says:

> Let the seeker approach the Master with reverent devotion.
> Then when he has pleased him by his humility, respect, and

service, let him ask whatever may be known about the *ātman*, the great Self.

Prashraya, respect or reverence, is the subject we'll take up tonight. One of the ways we show our respect for the Almighty, for the supreme Self, is by offering an invocation before beginning any kind of worship or any kind of work. This is an ancient practice. Invocation is a deep prayer from the heart, and it uplifts our actions by offering them to God and calling upon His grace. So, in the *Rig Veda*, the sages sing:

nama idugraṃ nama ā vivāse namo dādhāra pṛithivīm
uta dyām /
namo devebhyo nama īśha eṣhāṃ kṛitaṃ chideno
namasā vivāse //

Reverence to the Mighty One.
I adopt reverence as my offering.
Reverence holds earth and heaven in place.
Reverence to the Divine Ones.
With the power of reverence for the Lord,
May my lapses and inattention be purified. [6.51:8]

Baba Muktananda lived with great reverence for everything in God's creation. Respect was one of his principal teachings, respect for the Self that dwells within all things, sentient and insentient. In one of the question-and-answer sessions he held for seekers in the early days of the Ganeshpuri ashram, Baba said, "Every day during my lectures I say, respect everybody. To do this, first of all, you must respect yourself. Only then can you also respect others. You are not what you appear to be on the outside. You are something else on the inside, so discover that. Within a person there is the effulgence of God; each of you should see that radiance. Along with this light of God, there is so much joy. The purpose of human life is to attain that joy."

When did you begin to respect your parents? When did you stop respecting your parents? When did you begin to respect your schoolteachers? When did you stop? And your neighbors? When did your respect for your neighbors begin and when did it come to an end? When was the first time you felt respect for nature? And when did you stop regarding nature with respect?

Something to contemplate. It is very difficult to discern the moment when you first felt respect for yourself and others. But if you can discover when it was, then you will able to sustain that experience for the rest of your life. In the same way, if you can pinpoint the moment you stopped respecting the light within and without, in yourself and in others, in nature and in all the activities of this world, then you will know how to rekindle that power once again.

The power of respect is very strong. Please understand, we're not talking about etiquette. Many people are extremely polite . . . on the surface. Manners are a superficial thing. However, in most families, they are very important. Out of respect for your parents, you learn to be polite as a child, however reluctantly. You acquire good manners, partly because you're forced to, and you follow them because you want to please.

So many people remain "pleasers" all their lives. They want to please everybody. What can you call people like this? Puppies? You can't call them human beings because human beings have *viveka,* discrimination. They can understand, they have the power to think, to reflect on a situation or an impulse, to make distinctions. But these are just pleasers. They will do anything to please anyone. That is not what I mean by respect. Neither are good manners. I am talking about the respect that comes from the depth of your being because you have beheld the light in your own heart and, having embraced it within yourself, you are able to see the same light in others. Bearing that in mind, holding it in your consciousness, you respect others. Respect such as this is a profound form of love.

Light exists within everyone. Baba Muktananda continually said this. Over and again, he brought everyone's attention to the heart, so that each one might come to know his own light. To know your own light is to recognize God.

Once a seeker asked Baba, "How does one face a society that has no respect for spiritual incentive?" Baba answered, "We should not let the attitude of our society affect our mode of life, our ways, or our spiritual viewpoint. There can be only two reasons for a lack of spirituality—stupidity and egoism. If others are not willing to give up their egoism or stupidity, why should you give up your spiritual seeking?"

It is something to think about. If others are not willing to give up their skepticism, why should you give up your faith in God? It is so amazing! Why should a skeptic have more power than a believer? Which one of them is spineless? Now, in Kundalini yoga, in Siddha Yoga, we talk a great deal about the power of the spine. We say, "Elongate your spine, let it expand, sit tall." When you receive shaktipat, the Kundalini energy, which is dormant at the base of the spine, awakens and rises higher and higher. It travels up the *sushumnā nādī*, the central channel, and reaches the *sahasrāra* at the crown of the head. And there, this Shakti, this great energy, merges into the pure power of Consciousness, and you experience thousands of stars exploding, thousands of suns blazing. You are completely struck by this divine light. There is so much power, so much energy. It is stupendous! Despite all this, when believers hear something bad about God from people who don't believe in God, it is the believers who feel bad. Why? What makes you so weak?

Let me give you an example. Once two friends were walking down the street and they stopped at a newsstand so that one of them could buy a paper. The man thanked the vendor courteously. The vendor stared back at him, coldly, without a word of acknowledgment. "What a bad mood he's in," the other man commented.

"Oh, he's that way every night," his friend said.

"Then why are you so polite to him? Why do you keep coming here to buy your newspaper?"

And the man replied, "Why should I let him decide how I am going to act?"

When you let another person dictate your actions, it shows a definite lack of respect—not for your abilities, because you can still sing, you can still dance, you can still do your work. No, it is a sign that you have no respect for the light in your own heart, no faith in the Lord who dwells within you.

How does this happen? How does a person lose respect for himself or herself, for God, for creation, for Nature? In the Bible, it is written, "No one who practices deceit shall dwell in My house. No one who utters lies shall continue in My presence."

Earlier this evening you heard a talk about the power of spiritual practices. Over and over again, you are told, those practices keep the light burning. When you practice deception, however, you begin to lose respect for yourself, and gradually, your experience grows dim. Why? Because you cannot kid yourself. No matter how many justifications you come up with, you know what you are doing. Your heart, which wants to expand after shaktipat, begins to shrink and crumble. Your duplicity may be just a few words or a very small action. Nevertheless, over a period of time, this little deceit eats up your merit and the magnificent virtues begin to leave the realm of your heart.

So the 101st Psalm says, "No one who utters lies shall continue in My presence." People ask, "Is it true that a seeker can fall from grace? Is it true that once you receive shaktipat, it can disappear? Is it true that even after a person follows the spiritual path for many years, he or she can become deluded? Can something like that really happen?"

Yes, it is true. You fall from grace when you are not able to live up to the principles of the practices and your own greatest beliefs, when you lose touch with the goodness of your own heart, when you become insensitive to the presence of God. Then you do have the feeling of being far from grace. You may only be deceiving yourself in order to avoid pain. Even so, sooner or later, avoidance takes its toll. It feels as if grace has left you.

So you see it really doesn't matter how painful it is to face yourself and your actions honestly. Everyone's life is filled with pain and suffering. You cannot excuse yourself by saying, "Well, I am in pain; that's why I'm such an angry person, so volatile, so depressed," and so on. The fact is, as long as you have a body, you are subject to pain. You may slip and fall, and break your bones. Or you may eat one morsel of tainted food, unknowingly, and suffer for days on end until the poison leaves your body. Or perhaps your pain has been with you all your life. You may have been born with asthma, so that you can hardly breathe, your chest is constricted all the time and the pain is excruciating. Or you might have been born with a brain defect of some sort and live with a wretched headache all your life. Suffering is an inescapable part of the human condition. But it's really no excuse.

On the other hand, it is not true that grace ever leaves you. It is not true that, after shaktipat, Kundalini ever goes back to a dormant state. It is not true that you can lose God's love. Not ever. Not on your life. But when you stop respecting the awakened energy—by lying, for example—you begin to feel the lack of God's presence.

Let's take a very simple example. Many of you are here for a short time and you want to get the most out of it. You have heard of the glory of seva, selfless service. First of all, you've probably heard that you need great merit to perform seva, and that's true. Then, you know that by performing selfless service, you also acquire merit. So, naturally, you volunteer to go and do some form of seva—in the dishroom, or the garden, or in different offices, wherever. Maybe it's just welcoming people, saying hello.

On your way to your seva, you stop to chat with someone and you get completely caught up in the conversation. You think it's only going to be a few minutes. But it's such a *juicy* conversation. Mmm! You say, "Just five more minutes," and an hour goes by. You look at your watch, and you know you're supposed to arrive at your shift. Everybody is waiting for you. Everybody's counting on you. They trust you, they respect you, and you want to live up to that. But then you say, "I'll never get this chance again. I mean, the ball is rolling! I'm only here for a short while. Who knows when I'll see this friend again? Just five more minutes." Another two hours go by. Then you tell your friend, "You know, I have this seva. Do you think I should go?"

And your friend says, "It's up to you."

"Ohhh, of course, naturally, yes." Another hour goes by. In this way, many hours have gone by. Finally, you think, "What should I tell my seva supervisor? I know! I'll say, 'My hands were so... so *stiff*!' I mean the doctors did tell me, didn't they, not to use my hands... I'll say, 'You know, this is my holiday after all. I should be relaxing. I came here for a *retreat*! To be silent and totally absorbed in God. You don't know the pressure I'm under at home!' No, that sounds selfish. What can I say? Let me see. What did I do when I was ten years old... Remember, I got to school late, what really worked? No, it's too much. I'm not going back to childhood. This seva supervisor lives in the moment... Oh, I know! I will say that I thought so *many* people wanted to offer their services, why should I deprive them of the opportunity? Ahhh, that will work. There are so many people here, *they* need the merit, you know?"

Now this goes on. The story does not end here. It will never end. So the Bible says, "No man who utters lies shall continue in My presence." This doesn't mean God will abandon you. God never abandons anyone. Love never gives up on anyone. But by continually indulging in deception, by constantly telling lies, you destroy your own confidence. By performing such actions, you lose respect, inside and out. You let this magnificent virtue slip away.

In his book *Mukteshwarī*, Baba Muktananda said, "One who does not follow ashram dharma gets no respect in an ashram, even if he is trustworthy."

To follow ashram dharma, you must align yourself with the will of the Guru, the will of God, and the will of your own inner heart. To do this, you must watch your own mind. When you come across something in the ashram, what does your mind say? When you see something, hear something, feel something, what does your mind say? Is your mind able to absorb the shimmering Shakti? Is your being able to assimilate the love in a sacred place? Or does your mind kick in and squawk every inch of the way, whipping up one doubt after another? How does your mind act and react in an ashram? In your life in general? What is the state of your heart?

The American author Ralph Waldo Emerson said, "Men are respectable only as they respect." In the same vein, Confucius said, "If you respect others, others will respect you." In his book *Ashram Dharma*, Baba Muktananda said, "You will receive as much respect as you show to others. By honoring others, you are not doing a favor to them but to yourself."

When you acquire the ability to treat other people with respect, you yourself also gain confidence. You understand that, after all, you are a good person. Your heart is able to generate positive vibrations, positive thoughts. In this way, you become more established in your own goodness.

How must you approach a spiritual Master? A child? A king? A saint? A tree? A rock? An ocean? A mountain? Nature? How must you approach all beings, elements, animals? With respect. Then you receive everything. The awareness that gives birth to respect makes your heart expand, and the expanded heart receives all things: wisdom, love, knowledge, ever-increasing awareness—everything you need to live your life.

Baba Muktananda once said, "There are no evil forces as such. But we can create them. Since we create them, we can erase them. Rain falls from the sky, but evil forces are not created in that way. God does not create them for us; we create them for ourselves. Therefore, we should try to erase what we have created. If every person maintains respect for everyone else in his heart, all evil forces will disappear."

Baba's words ring with so much conviction. Evil forces germinate when there is no respect for man or God, no respect for nature, no respect for the elders or for the saints. These forces feed off that vacuum. They gain more and more power. True respect destroys them completely. Evil forces shy away from the power of reverence. When you have a great heart, no one can hurt you.

Your whole body also deserves your reverence. It holds the light of God. You are the custodian of this great light. With respect, protect it. Respect your body, your mind, and your heart. You must also respect time. You must respect your enemies as well as your friends. Respect the inhalation as it comes in and the exhalation as it goes out. The amount of respect you give to each element of life will be returned to you a hundredfold.

Above all, you are the custodian of this great heart that you have been given, and you must protect it. Let it be filled with respect. Respect for humanity, respect for nature, respect for the Master, and respect for God.

With great respect and great love, I welcome you with all my heart.

December 27, 1993

CHAPTER TEN

SELFLESS SERVICE

Sevā

WITH GREAT RESPECT AND GREAT LOVE, I welcome you all with all my heart.

Tonight, the moon is full. Because it's been overcast, we thought we wouldn't be able to see it. However, as I was walking to the hall for the evening program, I happened to look out the window and there was the full moon blazing. It was very beautiful. When the moon turns its face toward you, you do understand that it is the deity of the mind. The nectar of the moon makes the mind tranquil. Tonight, just as it was reaching its peak, you were all doing the *dhāranā*, the centering technique, of approaching the Self. The two processes were in complete harmony. The moon reached the fullest point of its nature just as you experienced yourselves coming closer and closer to your own inner Self, the greatest full moon of all. So nature outside and nature inside conspired. Somehow, when these two come together, it is easy to experience the presence of God.

In the last few evenings, we have expanded our discussion of the magnificent virtues to include the qualities that allow a seeker to approach a spiritual Master, a child, a king, a saint, a tree, a mountain, the ocean, God's world. We have been taking the help of a verse from the *Viveka Chūdāmani*, "The Crest Jewel of

Discrimination," in which the great Siddha Guru Shankaracharya gave seekers the key to pleasing the Master. Approach with reverence and devotion, he says. In that moment, if the Master sees that the seeker is ripe with the virtues of humility, respect, and selfless service, then all the seeker's questions will be answered, and he will be given the knowledge that is the Master's gift—knowledge of the *ātman*, Absolute Reality, his own indwelling Self.

Humility, respect, and seva, the virtues of a true seeker. Seva, selfless service, is a very deep and subtle subject. "The dharma of seva," says the *Pañchatantra*, "is mysterious and hard to understand. Even the yogis find it difficult to comprehend completely." Seva dharma, the high and righteous laws of selfless service, carefully observed, brings benefits that are often unexpected and almost impossible to put into words. Baba Muktananda thought of seva as a precious gift to seekers. He once remarked, "However dear a disciple may be to me, I insist on his working. And the dearer a person is, the more work I give him."

That is the blessing. Most of the actions that human beings perform in this world are tinged to some degree with selfishness, hatred, animosity, and pride. It's very rare for someone to be free of these things.

You always want something from the actions you perform, or else, through your actions, you want to have an effect on another person's life. You spend your time measuring the difference between your intention, your effort, and your reward. You always have a private agenda, an ulterior motive for the things you do, and you scarcely ever catch a glimpse of what it's like to be released from that burden. That is why it is said, without great merit, you cannot even come close to offering your service, and without blessings, you cannot achieve the state of heart that allows you to function selflessly.

Offering your work alone is not enough. The way you perform your work is crucial. In the *Bhagavad Gītā,* Lord Krishna makes three distinctions about actions and their value. He says:

anubandhaṃ kṣhayaṃ hiṃsām-anapekṣhya cha pauruṣham /
mohād-ārabhyate karma yat-tat-tāmasam-uchyate //

That action which is undertaken because of delusion,
disregarding its consequences, without a care for the loss
or injury to others,
and without considering one's own ability, is said to be
tamasic, filled with darkness. [18:25]

Jnaneshwar Maharaj comments on this, saying:

> Tamasic action is like the dark house of condemnation and the birthplace of all that is prohibited.
>
> A moth dazzled by a flame not only burns its body, but also prevents people from seeing the light.
>
> Similarly, this kind of action harms others as well as being useless and hurting the body.
>
> A tamasic person doesn't ask himself, What skills do I have? What opportunities are there? What is the advantage of doing this?

Of the three *gunas,* the three essential qualities by which our lives are colored, *tamas* is the darkest. *Rajas* is the quality which is mixed; it can be light and dark, pure and impure, at the same time, while *sattva* is the highest, the quality of goodness, purity, and light. In all the actions that people perform, these qualities succeed each other by turn, and it is a rare person who hasn't experienced all three at one time or another. However, some people's actions are completely saturated by *tamoguna*, the darkest quality. In other people, *rajoguna* predominates. Rajasic people have an insatiable desire to work and work. They put work itself to shame, not to mention what they do to their co-workers. And then there are the people whose every action is pure, whose every motivation is unselfish. In them, *sattva guna* is the prevailing quality.

In this verse, Lord Krishna is addressing tamasic actions, those which are undertaken out of delusion and without any regard for the consequences. A person who is filled with *tamoguna* is always thinking about himself. He has turned his being into a dungeon. Nothing can ever get through to him and he can never get out. Whatever he does or does not do, his attention is confined to his own interests, impulses, and desires.

As an example, let me tell you an anecdote that happened recently. One of the women who does seva outside the hall, helping people to get in and out comfortably, was speaking to someone else in the ashram.

She said, "This one fellow, who's been doing yoga for years, was about to go in the wrong door. I said, 'Please use the other door.' And he looked at me in this long-suffering way and rolled his eyeballs toward the ceiling. So to make him feel better, I said, 'Dharma. Seva dharma.'

"And he said, 'Oh come on. Red tape!' "

What is a person to think? Whenever somebody says or does anything like that, I always wonder, "What do they eat? What kind of food are they putting in their stomachs?" Because it is said in the Upanishads that the food a meditator eats must be very pure. In that way, you are able to have pure thoughts and feelings. On the other hand, if you cannot digest your food, you get a stomachache. The imbalanced churning of your digestive juices, combined with remnants of unhealthy food, gives rise to a toxic fume. And eventually it goes to the head. This is not something that only happened in Upanishadic times. When germs that should be processed by the intestines travel through the body, instead of being eliminated from the system, they disturb the cells of the brain. As a result, a person receives a very distorted impression of the world.

The scriptures declare that this world is a play of Consciousness. If a person cannot experience this—or even remember it—after quite a few years of spiritual practices, after all the karma that has been washed away by the Guru's grace and the fire of austerities, then this is the only conclusion you can reach. The pull of *tamoguna* is very strong. It is very dark.

The second kind of action that Lord Krishna discusses is that which is colored by *rajoguna*, the quality of passion and mixed motives. In chapter eighteen of the *Bhagavad Gītā*, Lord Krishna says:

yat-tu kāmepsunā karma sāhaṃkāreṇa vā punaḥ /
kriyate bahulāyāsaṃ tad-rājasam-udāhṛitam //

> But that action which is done out of longing
> for the fulfillment of desires or for gain,
> performed with selfishness or, again, with much effort,
> that is declared to be rajasic. [18:24]

Jnaneshwar Maharaj comments on this verse very beautifully. He says:

> He performs properly all those prescribed rites which will bring pleasurable results.
>
> He publicly boasts of having performed those ceremonies and makes them valueless by constantly speaking of them.
>
> Therefore, whatever a person does reverently, yet through egoism and the desire for the fruits of his action,
>
> It is like a rat burrowing through an entire mountain to find a single grain, or a frog stirring up the ocean for a little moss.

Haven't you ever felt this way? You want to perform selfless service, some action to bring about good, and you think, "I've got to do it! I've got to do it! I am doing it! I am doing it!" Whenever that happens, understand *rajoguna* is very active in your being, and you are perceiving yourself and the world through its lens. Entrenched in *rajoguna*, a person performs all his actions for pleasurable results, even the so-called "selfless" ones. These are the people who say, "I want work to be fun—that's when I can really give myself to it." *Rajoguna.*

Ask yourself this: just who is enjoying these pleasures? The ego. When the ego is fed, it experiences some kind of high. There are people who are unable to work without this state of elation. If there is a dip in their gratification, they find it difficult to perform any action at all. They feel, "Not a good day. I am not in the mood. No inspiration." Imagine what would happen if all the planets in the universe started thinking like that. "I don't feel like shining. Sun, keep your light away from me. It's not a good day..." If you don't want the planets to act that way, you should learn to keep an eye on yourself. Whenever you find yourself preoccupied by your demand for pleasure in your work, watch out.

The ancient philosophy of Vedanta compares this sort of pleasure-seeking to an itch: the sages say it can get you in a lot of trouble, if you constantly indulge in scratching it.

Do you remember the story? Once there was a blind man who was trapped in a prison cell. He was there for many days, many weeks. Finally, he heard a noise, a creaking sound and then a loud click. The lock on the door was turning. It was *open*! At that instant, *tamoguna* gave up on him and *rajoguna* took over his existence. Now, he wanted to perform the action of getting out of the cell. But how could he do it? He couldn't see where the door was. So, the blind man began to feel his way along the wall. He went all the way down one wall, found the corner, went all along the adjoining wall. But then a strange thing happened. Just when he was about to come to the door, he had an itch — and he scratched it. Of course, he kept walking as he scratched. By the time he put his hand back on the wall, he had gone right past the door.

He'd missed it. He didn't know that, of course. He just kept feeling his way along the walls. As soon as he came to the door again... it was the oddest thing... just a little itch. He took his hand off the wall and began to scratch. And, once again, he missed the door...

In this way, Vedanta says, an individual soul goes in circles, round and round, again and again. Every time there is a chance to become free from the bondage of his own limitations, he says, "Just one more sip... just one more time..."

The world is so enticing. Therefore, time after time, the individual turns away from freedom and blindly indulges in sense pleasures. The chance is right there. The door is open. The prisoner can walk out of the dungeon into a state of inconceivable freedom. No. He says, "Oh, my dear one... just let me give her one more kiss, and then I will be ready... just one more game... one more chance at the prize... just one more whatever...." But time keeps passing. The prisoner keeps walking. And there goes the door.

So it is that indulgence in a selfish pleasure gets you into trouble. All sorts of consequences arise from *rajoguna* — the desire for pleasurable results from your actions, doing one little thing and then saying, "Is this going to make me happy? Is this going to make me feel good?"

Haven't you noticed? Let's take a very simple example. You tell your spouse, "Oh, I love you so much." Your spouse is happy that you said it. He or she experiences joy at your expression of love and gratitude. But then you stand there, waiting. "Don't *you* want to say anything, dear?" *Rajoguna*. Always wanting praise, always wanting an action to produce pleasurable results.

Jnaneshwar Maharaj says, the person whose seva is performed in *rajoguna*, whose good actions are colored with these qualities of mixed motives, pleasure-seeking and passion, will always boast publicly about everything he's done. He wants the whole world to know what a good, spiritually evolved person he is. And yet, invariably, the kinds of happiness that can be found in *rajoguna* do not last.

A great German author, in speaking about the effect our attitude has on our actions, said, "It is not doing the thing we like to do, but liking the thing we have to do that makes life blessed."

The work is there. Selfless service can be performed at any time. How you apply yourself to it, how much of yourself you give is up to you. Are you going to walk through the ashram and experience, "So much Shakti, so much love. Let me go to the kitchen and see if I am fortunate enough to be needed. Let me go to the Seva Center and see if they have found all the people they need to insure the comfort and happiness of everyone here." Or are you going to go around, saying, "Red tape. Everyone's always telling me what to do."

How will you react? What is the state of your mind?

Baba Muktananda was very specific about the attitude you need to do seva properly. Your actions should be worthy of respect. You should perform respectful and noble actions so that people can learn something from you. Baba said, "Offer your service for the sake of service; do not have any other purpose."

In the *Bhagavad Gītā* Lord Krishna describes the third type of action as governed by sattvic or pure qualities, saying:

niyataṃ sañga-rahitam-arāga-dveśhataḥ kṛitam /
aphala-prepsunā karma yat-tat-sāttvikam uchyate //

> That action, which is prescribed by the scriptures,
> which is free from all attachments,
> performed without passion and without hate,
> by one who has no desire for any reward,
> is said to be sattvic or pure. [18:23]

In his commentary, Jnaneshwar Maharaj says,

> This daily duty, supported by periodic rites, is good and is like fragrance added to gold.
>
> Just as a mother will devote all the strength of her body and life to caring for a child without thinking of her own weariness,
>
> In the same way, a good person will perform his duty wholeheartedly, without a thought for its fruit, and by offering it to God.

Sattvic action. Last night I mentioned to one of the sevites that she seemed to be having a much easier time with her seva these days. In fact, all of the people she was working with had begun to function together very well as a team. "There is no anxiety in your seva anymore," I told her.

She smiled and said, "Yes, we have been meeting together before our seva begins. We practice some breathing techniques, we repeat the mantra and we do a *dhāraṇā.* We focus on the awareness that whatever seva we will perform tonight is in service to God and to the people who come to the ashram. Somehow, because of this, we are able to bring our love, and not nervousness, to our seva."

This is a sattvic approach to seva. You give the purity of your whole heart to it. You desire nothing from it. You have no expectation. You perform this service because you want to. You offer your effort to God, and so your heart is cleansed, your mind is cleansed, and you are able to experience the fruit of being in the ashram.

Everybody has to walk the spiritual path at his own pace. True understanding cannot be forced or given away; it has to grow organically in its own good time. Dharma, sadhana, selfless service, liberation—according to the scriptures, these are the highest purposes of human existence, and a lot of people need time to assimilate their meaning. On the other hand, their essence, like the presence of God, can be grasped in a single instant.

Once a young man fell madly in love with someone who did not return his affection. He was in such desperate shape that he couldn't think of anything else. He found no joy in anything. He was beside himself. Finally, one of his friends told him about a magician who lived on the outskirts of town. The young man went directly there and appealed to the magician for help.

The magician had dark eyes. They glowed with an unnatural light. He said, "If you really want me to help you, then you must follow my instructions to the letter."

"I will!" the young man cried. "I'll do anything! I just want to get over this awful feeling."

"Then," the magician said, "you must not say a single prayer for forty days, even in a crisis. Nor should you obey God in any way. Do not do any good deeds for anyone on earth. Above all, you must not mention God's name or give voice to any form of good intention. If you follow these instructions scrupulously, I shall be able to devise some bit of magic to achieve your goal."

The young man really wanted to get over this disease of infatuation and unrequited love. So he did everything the magician told him. In forty days, he returned to the dark, mysterious shack where the magician lived and paid a great deal of money, all he had, for a talisman. But it didn't work.

"You didn't follow my instructions," the magician said sourly. "Some good has come into being through you in the last forty days."

"I did nothing!" the young man protested. "I swear it! I went all forty days without thinking of God. I did no one a good turn. I did not say a single kind word. I refrained from making any sacred action. I ran from anything that came close to goodness. I give you my word."

"Think, my son, think. You must have done something, just a tiny thing. Otherwise, this talisman would work for you."

The young man shook his head. He went back over the last forty days but there was nothing, nothing he could think of that would break the spell . . . unless . . . All of a sudden, he said, "Could it be? One day, when I was walking down the road to work, I tripped over a rock. And I thought, 'I had better move this out of the way so nobody else trips and falls.' "

"Hah! That is a good action!" the magician said, and his voice grew stern. "Do not ridicule the God whose every command you slighted for forty days, and yet who, in His generosity, did not let this one small action go to waste."

These words sparked a fire in the young man's heart. It burned so high that it consumed his old infatuation in an instant and a new condition of love for God began to blaze within him. He went home and continued to practice his trade as a blacksmith, concealing the miracle that had changed his life. Every day he earned one dinar. Every night, he gave his earnings to the poor. But his heart was full and his happiness was perfect.

Because this state is within everyone's reach, Baba Muktananda, in his beautiful book *Reflections of the Self*, offers this priceless advice to seekers:

> Work as selflessly as the clouds
> that shower rain.
>
> With concentration,
> contentment and discipline,
> with great joy and ease,
> perform all your daily work.
> Still your mind; have no fear.
> Never invite anger.
> Perform your allotted tasks
> to please the Lord.
>
> If you serve your own Self with great joy,
> then you serve the entire world.

When you are able to accept the divine will, you are also able to give yourself completely to every tiny action in your life. Each one becomes a fragrant blossom; it becomes worthy of respect, and God adores you.

So, at the end of the *Bhagavad Gītā,* the great warrior Arjuna spoke to Lord Krishna. Arjuna said, "O Lord, as I have listened to you, again and again, all my doubts have vanished. My heart has become completely pure. And now, whatever I do, it is in your service. Whatever I think, it is in your service."

In Arjuna, the sense of doership had been removed. This is the key to selfless service. As long as you think "I am doing this, I am the doer of my action," your action loses all its power. When the ego has been purified and all doership abandoned, every action you perform has power.

The greatest servant of the Lord in the *Rāmāyana* and one of the most famous sevites of all times was Hanuman, the monkey-god, the son of the wind. Every gesture, every breath he drew was an expression of devotion. So, the Lord said to him,

> O Hanuman, for just one of the great services you have rendered to Me, I am bound to give you My very life. For the numerous other works you have performed in My name, I shall ever remain indebted to you.

How must you approach the Master, a child, a saint, a king, a tree, a mountain, an ocean, God's creation? With humility, respect, and the attitude of service. You must relinquish the thought "Give me! Give me what I want!" Instead, approach with the attitude "What can I give? What can I do for you?" That is when your heart opens. The thought "Give me" makes your heart contract, and in that state, there is nothing you can receive. In fact, even if a huge vessel of nectar were to be poured into your mouth, you would not be able to absorb it. Your heart could not contain it. That is exactly what happens to a lot of people. Therefore, why not change your outlook and seek to serve?

The great Indian poet Rabindranath Tagore said:

> I slept and dreamt that life was Joy,
> I awoke and saw that life was Service,
> I acted and behold, Service was Joy.

There is great bliss in selfless service. If, for any reason, you experience no joy when you do seva, it is usually for one of two reasons. One, your karmas are being washed away. You are in the process of doing sadhana and though you may not yet derive joy from your seva, good things are happening. Joy will come. The second possibility is this: you may not be giving yourself completely to your service. Maybe you are full of expectations and they are getting in the way. It is usually one or the other of these factors that is interfering, holding joy at bay.

Most of you are only able to come to the ashram for a few weeks or a few months at a time. You make a great effort to come here; you save, you plan, you travel long distances. Now that you are here, get the most out of your stay. Treat the ashram as a place for contemplation, for the study of the Self, for chanting, meditation, seva, receiving God's grace. Renew your own heart, renew the energy in your own mind. Treat this as a sacred place. Then you will notice you are having a very joyful experience. You are able to see God's face in a hostess—and not red tape.

As you have come to understand in the last few evenings, the virtues mentioned in the *Viveka Chūdāmani* help you to approach the Master by changing your experience of your own Self. As you experience humility, your mind becomes supple and your heart expands with love. As you experience respect, your heart expands even more and limitations begin to fall away. As you perform one kind action for another human being, with an attitude of selflessness and service, your whole being is filled with unearthly joy. When you have imbibed these virtues fully, you will know, as Shankaracharya said, whatever may be known about the *ātman*, the great Self, the Supreme Being who dwells within you.

With great respect and great love, I welcome you all with all my heart.

December 28, 1993

CHAPTER ELEVEN

THE PURE HEART

WITH GREAT RESPECT AND LOVE, I welcome you all with all my heart.

My Guru, my Master, Baba Muktananda, reintroduced Siddha Yoga to the modern world. In *Secret of the Siddhas*, the book in which he expounded the philosophy of Kashmir Shaivism, he said, "Siddha Yoga is the teaching of those great beings who had fully attained the Truth and who had become one with Paramashiva, the all-pervasive Consciousness and supreme Guru. This field of knowledge is beyond human ambition, beyond the mind and imagination. It is a venerable path to the realization of Truth. We follow it seeking the supreme love of our own inner Consciousness."

How do we draw near to the goal of our seeking? As an answer to that, we have turned to a line from a poem by one of the saints, "My Lord loves a pure heart." This sublime phrase, this song of the soul, is a message to all human beings. It is an invitation to those who are just setting out on the spiritual path and an inspired piece of advice for anyone already walking the path to God.

The words come from Kabir, an enlightened Master who lived in the fifteenth century, in Benares, one of the holiest cities of India. Very little is known about Kabir's life. His birth was not recorded and his whole existence is surrounded by legend. Most of what we know about him we have learned from his poems, and they rarely describe the circumstances or events of his life. Kabir sang about the inner worlds. He was tireless also in his efforts to help Hindus and Muslims live together in harmony. In fact, to this day, Hindus believe Kabir was a Hindu and the Muslims claim him as a Muslim. But the truth is, no one really knows what Kabir's religious preference was. He embraced the Lord and gave his love to everyone with absolute purity.

All this is contained in the poem which gave us our title. Kabir says:

> Rama, the Lord, has possessed me.
> Hari, the beloved Lord, has enchanted me.
> All my doubts have flown like birds migrating in winter.
> When I was mad with pride,
> The Beloved did not speak to me.
> But when I became as humble as ashes,
> The Master opened my inner eye,
> Dyeing every pore of my being in the color of love.
> Drinking nectar from the cup of my emptied heart,
> I slept in His abode in divine ecstasy.
> The devotee meets the Lord like gold merging with its luster.
> My Lord loves a pure heart.

This universe is magnificent. It is also an endless circle. Without the clarity of a pure mind and heart, it is difficult to tell where good days begin and bad days end — or vice versa. The world goes around and around, and so do most people. Almost everyone leads his life against a background of confusion and the struggle for meaning. What is life? What is the worth of a human being? Why live? Why does one die?

There are many other questions. For instance, why accumulate possessions? And how do you lose them? Why do you have relatives? And then, why do you lose them? Why do you fall in love? Why do you get rejected? Why do you fall out of love? So many whys, so many hows — endless circles.

The century in which Kabir lived was also turbulent. People of different religions despised one another and destroyed one another, all in the name of God. So, it was extremely significant when someone like Kabir disengaged himself from these unending conflicts and experienced the true purpose of life.

In the first lines of his poem, Kabir says, "Rama, the Lord, has possessed me. Hari, the beloved Lord, has enchanted me." This is not something that happens by accident. Kabir gave himself to the highest authority, to the highest power. He allowed himself to be enchanted by the Lord.

It took a great deal of courage in those days to turn one's back on the conventions of race and caste. It was much more convenient, much less dangerous to go along with the old arguments and take sides. But it was not God's way, and God was what Kabir wanted. So when he says "My Lord loves a pure heart," Kabir is speaking from experience. He struggled and he strived. He makes it very clear: to know ecstasy, to know God's beauty, God's love, your heart has got to be immaculate and very strong. Love itself is so pure that only a pure heart can sustain the experience of it.

My Guru, Baba Muktananda, was a living embodiment of dharma, and he was adamant on this subject. In *Reflections of the Self*, Baba wrote:

> Never compromise your purity;
> perfect it within and without.
> Be as radiant as the sun,
> have love as fresh as the moon,
> be as clear as spotless crystal.

A fainthearted person always tries to bargain with life. He swims in an undercurrent of argument and complaint, constantly trying to negotiate a better deal. Are you like that? Have you ever said "I took the time to go to a holy place twice. Why isn't my life better?" Or are you like the one who says "I'm not such a bad person. Why do people treat me unkindly?" Or "I've repeated the mantra so many times, why do I still feel restless?"

The other day, someone said, "I thought Siddha Yoga was my

whole life. And now, when I'm going through a crisis, I want to know, why aren't the teachings holding me up? Why do I still feel bad?" This is the way fainthearted people compromise the goodness of their practices. If one thing goes wrong, they begin to sabotage their whole sadhana. They squander the merit they have acquired. Baba Muktananda states very clearly, "Never compromise your purity." What does that mean? For one thing, it means that you don't deny all your experiences just because of some passing difficulties.

Baba insisted on lasting purity within and without, unflinching purity. He also said that this virtue can come quickly to anyone who longs for it. "Just as a person can fall from purity in a single moment, an impure person can become pure in a moment, through repentance," Baba said. "The Lord does not judge whether you are pure or impure. He only sees the quality of your heart, the devotion you feel. Nor does the Lord bestow grace on anyone. It is the devotee himself who draws God's grace through his effort and his devotion."

This is a very significant line. "It is the devotee himself who draws God's grace through his effort and his devotion." In the *Bhagavad Gītā*, Lord Krishna says further:

samo'haṃ sarva bhūteṣhu na me dveṣhyo 'sti na priyaḥ /
ye bhajanti tu māṃ bhaktyā mayi te teṣhu chāpy aham //

I am the same in all beings;
To me there is none hateful or dear;
But those who worship Me with devotion are in Me,
And I am also in them. [9:29]

So, whenever you catch yourself thinking or saying "Why am I not receiving God's love?" try to remind yourself not to look outside for the answer. You must look at your own heart. Similarly, if you find yourself saying "Why am I not receiving any love from my own child?" look inside and see how much love you are giving. What are you feeling? What are you thinking? What is the state of your heart?

"The heart" is such a broad term, it carries a slightly different meaning for every individual. Still, everyone knows the heart is precious, and that, when something comes from the heart, it is honest, it is very real. So to a certain degree everyone does recognize that the heart is a sacred place and not something to be trifled with. The heart must be cherished. The heart deserves justice. A Spanish author once said, "Trust your heart. It is the oracle that foretells what is most important. Trust your heart."

Some intellectuals like to claim that they can only be affected by reason and logic. They place themselves above the domain of the heart which, to them, is only for sentimental, feebleminded people who don't know how to think. But they still get hurt when they don't get what they want, and their hearts still ache when they are ignored. Whatever these people may say, they are still subject to the pain of the heart, and they are still entitled to know the ecstasy of love.

When the heart opens, it doesn't ask the mind's permission. The heart may not be logical. But it has a power which sends the mind reeling in bliss.

All religious texts and philosophical works attach great importance to the heart. In the physical body, once the heart stops, life is finished. In the spiritual body, once the heart is awakened, a greater life begins. So, in both the mundane and the spiritual sense, the role of the heart is vast and the power of the heart is acknowledged as a great mystery.

Sometimes scientists come to the ashram and try to analyze everything according to the standards of Western science. Many of them ask if the Kundalini Shakti can be monitored by machines, and I answer, "Are you married?"

"Yes, I am," they say. Or "I have a girlfriend or a boyfriend." Invariably, they say one or the other, and then I ask, "Has your machine registered your love for him or for her?"

"Oh," they say, "very interesting."

Then I tell them, "When you succeed in monitoring your love for your beloved on a machine, you can come back and ask me about measuring the Kundalini Shakti."

Right now, let us take a few minutes to savor what the sages of the Upanishads say about the heart. The sages speak with the voice of the inner Self. The truths that were revealed to them in meditation became the scriptures, the oral tradition which has come down to us from Master to disciple. In fact, the word *upanishad* means "to sit close to the teachings, with keen devotion." That is also why these verses have the power of *dhāranās*, the centering techniques of yoga. By focusing your mind on these words and also by relishing them, you invoke the experience that inspired them.

The *Katha Upanishad* says:

aṅgushṭha-mātraḥ purusho jyotirivādhūmakah /
īśhāno bhūta-bhavyasya sa evādya sa u śhvaḥ etad vai tat //

A Being the size of a thumb dwells in the center of the body like a flame without smoke. This Being is the Lord of the past and the future. He is the same today and tomorrow. This Being is truly Thạt. [2.1:13]

The *Katha Upanishad* also says:

taṃ durdarśhaṃ gūḍham-anupravishṭaṃ guhāhitaṃ
gahvareshṭhaṃ purāṇam /
adhyātma-yogādhigamena devam matvā dhīro
harsha-śhokau jahāti //

Realizing through meditation the primordial God who is difficult to see, deeply hidden, set in the cave of the heart, dwelling in the deep, the wise person goes beyond both joy and sorrow. [1.2:12]

The *Kaivalya Upanishad* says:

pareṇa nākāṃ nihitaṃ guhāyām
vibhrājad etad yatayo viśhanti

The Supreme is higher than the heavens,
yet it shines in the cave of the heart.
Those who strive for it, enter into it. [3]

In every respect, from the ordinary to the sublime, the quality of your heart is what matters most. To live a decent life you have to have a good heart. If you want to know God, you have to have a heart that is pure as well as steady, one that is capable of holding grace and never wavers from its purpose. Even after the physical body perishes, truly, the heart is what lives on. The one thing you never forget about someone who has died is your love for that person and that person's love for you.

All the virtues of a human being come from a pure heart, and on some level, everyone knows this. As soon as you do something uplifting, generous, or altruistic, people speak about your heart. "What a warm, kindhearted person he is!" they say. "What a generous heart she has!" "She has a heart of gold." "His heart is in the right place." People who are fun to be around are lighthearted, heroes are lionhearted — haven't you ever heard that expression?— and some people, though old in years, are young at heart. "The heart of a saint," says Tukaram Maharaj, "is as soft as butter."

It is interesting to see how good qualities are usually associated with the heart and negative ones with the mind. For instance, the heart never schemes or plots to get its own way. The heart never looks for its own advantage or takes pleasure in anyone's pain. The heart melts. It overflows. Its very nature is pure and its natural inclination is toward kindness, love, generosity, valor, compassion, forgiveness, innocence, righteousness, and honesty — to name just a few. The heart is free from illusions. Illusions are an epidemic of the mind.

Saint Augustine said, "To my God, a heart of flame. To my fellowmen, a heart of love. To myself, a heart of steel." Allow this understanding of the vastness of the heart to be a torch to guide you on the path of Siddha Yoga. "My Lord loves a pure heart."

Baba Muktananda had explored the inner mysteries of the heart in meditation and so he could say, "In this heart, God dwells; it is the real shrine of the Lord. The light of God shimmers in the heart, scintillating and vibrating all the time. Through meditation you can see this light, and when the inner Shakti has unfolded, you merge into it. It is there for you to find. It is yours."

The day I received shaktipat, my destiny took a new turn. My life became an adventure and my fortune blossomed. Soon afterwards, I was meditating in the Cave in the Ganeshpuri Ashram. If you have never been to Gurudev Siddha Peeth in Ganeshpuri, India, let me tell you that there is a large, cool, dark room there that is reserved for meditation; we call it the Cave. Now, every particle of dust in that ashram is alive with the love of God. Even so, the Cave is special. So many seekers have meditated there. The moment you walk into that velvety darkness, you feel the power of their aspiration and their absorption in the ecstasy of the heart. What's more, the Cave is located directly under Baba's house. The energy of meditation is so intoxicating there that you are drawn inside as soon as you sit down.

On that particular day, I sat down right in front of the altar. I bowed to Bhagawan Nityananda's picture and then I closed my eyes. As I was meditating, I saw a light in my heart. It appeared all of a sudden. It was a white flame, no bigger than the tip of a finger, but so brilliant that it started illuminating everything, absolutely everything. The *Guru Gītā* talks about *aṅgushṭha-mātra-purushạm*, a being who is the size of a thumb in the region of the heart, a being made of light.

At first, I just sat there watching it, becoming more and more ecstatic, and then it was as if my mind clicked in with a doubt. I thought, "Is this really happening? Or am I just imagining it? Am I just wishing it would happen?"

Immediately the light became dimmer and smaller. I got really frightened, I thought I had destroyed it, and so, naturally, I turned to Baba. "Oh Baba, maybe I wasn't hallucinating after all, maybe the light was real!" Right in the middle of this incredible experience, I was having a conversation with my mind. It is so amazing sometimes how present your mind can be, with its foolish remarks, and yet the experience continues. The light in my heart kept getting smaller and smaller. I realized I could just fall into that darkness and be lost in it forever. So I began to pray, "Baba, oh Baba, please don't let it go out! Please keep the flame burning!"

As soon as this prayer came up, though I was still in meditation, I saw Baba's form appear. He moved toward the altar in the Cave and picked something up from beneath Bhagawan Nityananda's picture. I couldn't really see what it was—a vessel or container of some kind. He came over to me and began pouring something clear as oil into my heart. It felt very, very cool. As this substance was being poured into me, the flame began to blaze again. To this day, I can still feel the sensation of its warmth in my heart.

The flame in the heart protects you. Baba talked about this flame a great deal. Sometimes he called it the flame of love. It is a fact. A brilliant white flame is burning inside you, in the mind, in the intellect, in the words you read and the people you see. When you perceive it, when you uncover it, the great statements of the scriptures become real for you: "I am the Truth." "God dwells within me." Without the experience of the Truth, in the cave of the heart, these are just phrases, just empty words. You must see it for yourself.

All the great beings spend their lives gazing at this inner light. It is like the steady flame of a lamp in a place where there is no wind. It is extremely brilliant. It shimmers and yet, at the same time, it is utterly still, magnificent to watch. This is the flame of your own inner Self, passionless and pure. Nothing is making it burn. Nothing can extinguish it. In the *Yoga Sūtras*, Patanjali says this flame is beyond all sorrow. It is the goal of all striving, the source of all the happiness in the world. So great is the human heart.

Then what can Kabir possibly mean by saying the Lord loves a *pure* heart? In and of itself, the heart is unblemished, free from limitations, free from painful memories. When it comes to the heart, how can you speak of impurity?

Perhaps we can begin to think about it by asking ourselves a question or two. For example, why do you feel a pain in the region of the heart every now and then? The heart is sublime. It holds the flame of God. It is His kingdom. Then why do you sometimes feel as though your heart is being squeezed or wrung until it is totally dry? Why do you sometimes feel you are losing heart? Or that your heart is breaking? Where is the impurity?

Picture the heart surrounded by a hard thick shell of impurities. Think of it like a living thing trapped inside a rock. Do you begin to see? Sometimes one truth is shrouded by many theories, making it very difficult to perceive. In the same way, the heart is encased by impurities, by the impressions of past actions and the ravages of the six enemies—anger, lust, pride, jealousy, delusion, and greed. The debris of all the pleasures of this world collects in the region of the heart as well. So do all the unclear, unresolved events of life, anxieties about the future, and lack of purpose.

So the notion of impurity applies not to the kernel of the heart, but to the layers around it. You might call these layers the courtyard of the heart. A great German mystic, Meister Eckhart, describes it like this: "A man has many skins in himself covering the depths of his heart. Why, thirty or forty skins, as thick and hard as the hide of an ox or a bear, cover the soul."

How do we get rid of this shell? How do we go beyond the courtyard and enter the heart itself?

The only way this can be done is through spiritual practices. Performing spiritual practices is like going to the source of the stream of Consciousness. There, the water is crystal clear, refreshing, and life-giving. By drinking this pure, shining energy, your mental faculties are rejuvenated. You feel new again and that is part of being alive. You must experience the newness of your own being again and again. If the freshness of life is destroyed, you lose interest in it. But if you feel new and fresh, life is exhilarating. You want to live, you want to know, you want to do something for humanity.

The teachings of the Siddhas invoke this, your own inner power. With the help of their pure thoughts, you begin to discover your own innate goodness. That is the whole point of spiritual practices: recognizing *your* goodness, understanding your own glory. In meditation, you find your own way of knowing and experiencing the truth of your own heart.

When you dip a flower in gold, it lasts forever. When you bathe the mind in contemplation of the divine, it gains everlasting purity.

"My Lord loves a pure heart." Going through the scriptures and texts of many different traditions, it is always amazing to see how much emphasis there is on the pure heart and pure mind in all religions and cultures. In fact, if God dwells in the heart, the mind is the gateway to knowledge of Him. When you become aware of the way your mind thinks, the way your intellect judges, the way your ego parades around; when you become aware of how your subconscious mind retains all the impressions of your thoughts and actions, then you come to understand the necessity of spiritual practices. The effort it takes to cleanse the psychic instruments becomes very precious to you.

The *Philokalia* is a collection of writings from the Fathers of the Greek Orthodox Church. It says, "The ultimate goal of our profession, our seeking, our faith is the kingdom of God. Its immediate purpose, however, is purity of heart, for without this purpose we cannot reach our goal. We should therefore always have this purpose in mind; and should it ever happen that for a short time our heart turns aside from the direct path, we must bring it back again at once. We must keep guiding our lives with reference to our ultimate purpose, as if it were a carpenter's rule."

It is the natural tendency of the mind to wander. However, a seeker should become sensitive to this and keep bringing the mind and the heart back to the right path.

So spiritual practices are a continual reminder as well as a source of strength. A reminder of what? Of your own greatness. You are great. That is the truth, whether you know it or not. It is up to you to recognize it, to realize the value of the One who dwells in your heart.

Isn't it amazing how blind you can be to your own immense goodness? If you only knew . . . Isn't it time you found out? Your own greatness is much stronger than your bad habits. It is only when you let yourself get carried away by the pull of bad habits that you feel helpless. Can't you understand? You are the master of your senses. You are the landlord of the field that you have been given in the form of this body. Don't you see? You are the caretaker as well as the inhabitant. Isn't it clear? You are in control. You are so great that everything you ever wished for is right in the palm of your hand.

Isn't it time you came into possession of your kingdom?

With great respect, with great love, I welcome you all with all my heart.

November 27, 1993

In the End, Love

WITH GREAT RESPECT AND GREAT LOVE, I welcome you all with all my heart.

Very soon, another season of the year will come to an end. The theme of this summer in South Fallsburg, as most of you know, was cultivating the magnificent virtues. We were able to explore many of the virtues named by Lord Krishna in the *Bhagavad Gītā*, and we managed to contemplate quite a few of them. You can continue to study the *Bhagavad Gītā* and the luminous commentary called *Jñāneshwarī*, by Jnaneshwar Maharaj. Some people tell me they have read chapter sixteen many, many times since we began. They also read the commentary again and again. It is very pleasing and rewarding to know that people do try to follow what is said in the programs. Sometimes, you wonder if the teachings go in one ear and out the other. However, when people tell you things like that, you realize, no, the teachings go straight to the heart; and they stay there.

In the beginning, love. In the end, love. In the middle, we have to cultivate virtues. A devotee of the Lord expressed his love in a very beautiful prayer. He said:

> May this thread of love that connects me to You never break,
> O Lord.

Since the day I gave my heart to You, I am beside myself
with ecstasy.
Like someone mad with love, I roam about dancing.

Your song has awakened my love,
And this love has touched off an extraordinary pain in
my heart.
These eyes of mine are filled with the vision of You.
I can never forget Your exquisite beauty.

Having been through worldly relationships, I have come to
Your door.
O Lord, please don't reject me, for I have taken refuge in You.
You are the only one who enchants my heart.
Only You can remove my pain.

We must learn to let love grow in our lives. Soon you will be returning to your different roles and responsibilities in the world. The retreat in South Fallsburg gave you a short break from all that, but now you must go back and fulfill your dharma. Every year, as this time approaches and people prepare to resume their lives in the world, they come to me and ask, "Gurumayi, do you have a final message for me? Something for me personally, just a few words that will give me a direction to follow in the months to come?"

There is one simple verse in the *Mahābhārata,* the great epic of India, that contains the essence of all its teachings on dharma. I want you to take this verse with you. This verse is the final message... for the time being. It is for everyone.

The *Mahābhārata* says:

dharmo jayati nādharmaḥ satyaṃ jayati nānṛitam /
kṣhamā jayati na krodhaḥ kṣhamāvān brahmaṇo bhavet //

Dharma, righteousness, always wins, never unrighteousness.
Truth is always victorious; untruth always fails in the end.
Patience, forbearance, always wins out, not anger.
One who is patient becomes established in the Absolute,
in Brahman.

The word for *patience* in the Sanskrit language is *kshamā*. It is very interesting, the same word also means "forgiveness." One who is patient becomes established in the Absolute. You must have patience to forgive. If you can forgive, that means you are very patient. *Kshamā*, like dharma, is a very beautiful word.

This year, it seems, we talked a lot about increasing our "saint time"—the amount of time we devote to dharma. This is one of the questions that troubles people most. They always want to know, "What is my dharma?" The answer is very clear: The true dharma of every human being is to know his own Self. You have to get your priorities straight. If you keep this goal in sight, then everything else falls in line with it. One thing follows another as naturally as the seasons, without your having to worry about it.

All summer long we focused on the virtues which the sages call our divine wealth, and an extraordinary thing happened. People who were not able to come to South Fallsburg followed the teachings wherever they were. We received many, many letters from people who were translating the magnificent virtues into action in Australia, in India, in South America, in Europe, in Japan. Their experiences were very beautiful. In fact, sometimes it seemed that people in all those places learned as much, or more, from the retreat as the people here in the ashram did.

Now, you will also begin to realize how much you have imbibed. While you were here, totally immersed in an ocean of self-effort and grace, you may not have been able to notice how much you were changing, how many virtues you were acquiring. But when you go home again, you'll see. You may be sitting quietly in your room or driving to your office, and all of a sudden, it will hit you. "What happened to the two pebbles I could never get out of my heart? They are not there anymore. What happened to the thorns?" Every time your heart was touched, you used to feel sharp thorns and now, all of a sudden, you realize they are not there anymore. You see somebody at home or at work and you ask yourself, "Why don't I hate that person? Why am I not angry? What's happened? Who has changed?"

In this way, you will come across many surprises about yourself. You will notice that a great transformation has taken place. You are experiencing exquisite love. You are experiencing sweet thoughts. For the first time in your life, you feel you have a green thumb. Whatever you touch, grows. Whatever you undertake, something positive comes out of it. You feel like you have golden feet. Wherever you go, the atmosphere brightens and begins to shine.

So, you may not notice a great change while you are here in the ashram for a month or two, or a week or two, or even for a day or two. But when you are back home, you will definitely see the difference. The same thing is true for the people who are staying on in the ashram. Once their friends and fellow sevites have gone, they will also begin to notice how many changes have taken place inside them, and in the way they live. You do need some time to yourself in order for the changes to register.

So have faith.

The *Tao Te Ching* presents the wisdom of the Chinese sages about the Self. In one of the verses, Lao Tsu says:

> The wise student hears of the Tao and practices it diligently.
> The average student hears of the Tao and gives it thought
> now and again.
> The foolish student hears of the Tao and laughs aloud.
> If there were no laughter, the Tao would not be what it is.
>
> Hence it is said:
> The bright path seems dim;
> Going forward seems like retreat;
> The easy way seems hard;
> The highest Virtue seems empty;
> Great purity seems sullied;
> A wealth of Virtue seems inadequate;
> The strength of Virtue seems frail;
> Real Virtue seems unreal;
> The perfect square has no corners;
> Great talents ripen late;
> The highest notes are hard to hear;
> The greatest form has no shape;

The Tao is hidden and without name.
The Tao alone nourishes and brings everything to fulfillment.

There *is* hope. If you think you haven't cultivated all the virtues you heard about, understand, one day they will shine inside you. Baba said: "These great qualities exist inside you. It's just a matter of time until they reveal themselves. When they do, you will recognize them immediately as your own. And then, as they begin to grow and grow and grow, you will experience contentment."

Everything is filled with the most sublime peace and well-being; and you will experience that, too, in the fullness of time. Practice cultivating these virtues and putting them into action. So much will happen. So many things will come to you—things that you have always wanted to do and have never been able to manage.

These magnificent virtues give you a lot of faith in yourself.

Always remember this: in the beginning, love; in the middle, virtues; and in the end, love once again. Whatever is happening, keep love in sight. It is the supreme goal. Whether you are fighting, or having a hard time, whether you are suffering, going through a difficult financial period, breaking up a relationship, struggling in your profession—however rough things may get, keep love in sight. Love in the beginning and love in the end. Allow your love for God to shimmer everywhere you look, in everything you touch. Never lose sight of love. Even if you don't feel love in the entire region of the heart, in your entire head, in your entire being—let there be a tiny spot, just one tiny spot in your being that throbs with love. Never let it vanish. Never cover it up, or stifle it. Always stay in touch with it. Let it fill your eyes.

Let this be your highest dharma. After having heard so much, said so much, done so much, only one thing remains, and that is love. Allow this love to shine in your being. Just a tiny spot. That will be plenty. It will take you across.

With great respect, with great love, I welcome you all with all my heart.

Sadgurunāth Mahārāj kī Jay!

August 30, 1993

Note on Sources

Many of the quotations from scriptures have been freshly rendered, drawing from the following sources in English, in addition to the original Sanskrit texts:

Kripananda, Swami. *Jnaneshwar's Gītā.* Albany: State University of New York Press, 1989

Radhakrishnan, S. *The Principal Upanishads.* Atlantic Highlands, NJ: Humanities Press, 1992

Singh, Jaideva. *The Yoga of Vibration and Divine Pulsation.* Albany: State University of New York Press, 1992

Sivananda, Swami. *Bhagavad Gītā.* Durban, South Africa: The Divine Life Society of South Africa, 1983

Verses from *Shrī Avadhūta Stotram* and *Devy-Aparādha-Kṣhamāpana-Stotram* are taken from translations which appear in *The Power of Chanting*, published by Gurudev Siddha Peeth, Ganeshpuri, India.

The following quotations are reproduced by permission of the publishers:

Guide to Sanskrit Pronunciation

Vowels

Sanskrit vowels are categorized as either long or short. In English transliteration, the long vowels are marked with a bar above the letter and are pronounced twice as long as a short vowel. The vowels 'e' and 'o' are also pronounced like long vowels.

Short:	Long:
a as in c*u*p	*ā* as in c*a*lm
i as in g*i*ve	*ī* as in s*ee*n
u as in f*u*ll	*ū* as in sch*oo*l
e as in s*a*ve	*ai* as in *ai*sle
o as in ph*o*ne	*au* as in c*ow*
ṛi as in w*ri*tten	

Consonants

The main variations from the way consonants are pronounced in English are the aspirated consonants. These are pronounced with a definite *h* sound. In particular, *th* is not pronounced like the English *th* as in *th*rone, nor is *ph* pronounced as in *ph*one. They are pronounced as follows:

kh as in in*kh*orn	*ṅ* as in si*ng*
gh as in lo*gh*ut	*ñ* as in ca*ny*on
jh as in he*dgeh*og	*ṇ* as in no*n*e
ṭh as in boa*th*ouse	*n* as in s*n*ake
th as in an*th*ill	*śh* as in bu*sh*
ḍh as in roa*dh*ouse	*ṣh* as in *sh*un
dh as in a*dh*ere	*kṣh* as in au*ct*ion
ph as in loo*ph*ole	*ṃ* is a nasal *m*
bh as in a*bh*or	*ḥ* is an aspiration

For a detailed pronunciation guide, see *The Nectar of Chanting*, published by SYDA Foundation.

Glossary

Abhayam [*abhayam*]
The divine quality of fearlessness, a state of steadfast virtue in which one is not swayed by the fear-born inner enemies: delusion, desire, anger, lust, pride, greed, and envy.

Action, the yoga of
The yogic discipline of offering all physical, verbal, and mental actions as worship; the practice of surrender and nondoership. *See also* yoga, seva.

Akrodha [*akrodha*]
Absence of anger, freedom from anger; the virtuous discipline of renouncing anger.

Arati [*āratī*]
A ritual act of worship during which a flame, symbolic of the individual soul, is waved before the form of a deity, sacred being, or image that embodies the divine light of Consciousness. Arati is preceded by the sound of bells, conches, and drums, and accompanied by the singing of a prayer.

Arati Karun [*āratī karūṅ*]
The name of the prayer written by one of Swami Muktananda's devotees, that is customarily sung in Siddha Yoga ashrams after the *Guru Gītā*.

Arjuna [*arjuna*]
Third of the five Pandava brothers and one of the heroes of the *Mahābhārata*; considered to be the greatest warrior of all. He was the friend and devotee of Lord Krishna. It was to Arjuna that Lord Krishna revealed the knowledge of the *Bhagavad Gītā*.

Ashram [*āśhrama*]
(*lit.* a place that removes the fatigue of worldliness) The abode of a Guru or saint; a monastic place of retreat where seekers engage in spiritual practices and study the teachings of yoga.

Ashram dharma [*āśhrama dharma*]
Right action in relation to ashram life; the inner posture and behavior that allow a person to devote himself or herself to the high attitude and disciplines of ashram life. *See also* dharma.

Ashvatthama [*aśhvatthāmā*]
The fiery son of Drona; kin of the Kaurava family in the *Mahābhārata*.

Atharva Veda [*atharva veda*]
One of the four primary scriptures of ancient India (which were shruti, "heard," by inspired rishis, seers). Protective healing formulas and prayers predominate in the *Atharva Veda*. *See also Rig Veda*; *Sāma Veda*; *Yajur Veda*; Vedas.

Atma-jnana [*ātma-jñāna*]
Knowledge of the supreme Self.

Atman [*ātman*]
Divine Consciousness residing in the individual; the supreme Self; the soul.

Atma sakshatkara [*ātma sākśhatkāra*]
(*lit.* to see the Self) The direct experience of the supreme Self; Self-realization.

Atma vichara [*ātma vichāra*]
The practice of inquiring into the nature of the Self.

Austerities
See tapasya.

Avadhuta [*avadhūta*]
An enlightened being who lives in a state beyond body-consciousness and whose behavior is not bound by ordinary social conventions.

Avadhuta Stotram [*avadhūta stotraṃ*]
A hymn chanted in Siddha Yoga ashrams in praise of Bhagawan Nityananda, the great Siddha and avadhuta who was Baba Muktananda's Guru.

Awakening
See Shaktipat.

Baba, babaji [*bābā*]
(*lit.* father) A term of affection and respect for a saint, holy man, or father. *See also* Muktananda, Swami.

Baba Muktananda
See Muktananda, Swami.

Bhagavad Gita [*bhagavad gītā*]
(*lit.* Song of the Lord) One of the world's spiritual treasures; an essential scripture of Hinduism; a portion of the *Mahābhārata*, in which Lord Krishna instructs his disciple Arjuna on the nature of God, the universe, and the supreme Self, on the different forms of yoga, on the nature of dharma, and the way to attain liberation.

Bhagawan [*bhagawān*]
(*lit.* the Lord) That which is glorious, divine, venerable, and holy; a form of address for God or saints; a term of great honor. Baba Muktananda's Guru is known as Bhagawan Nityananda. *See also* Nityananda, Bhagawan.

Bhajan [*bhajan*]
An Indian devotional song in praise of God.

Bhartrihari [*bhartṛihari*]
A legendary renunciant, poet, and sage; a king who gave up his throne to become a yogi; the collection of his poems is known as the *Shatakatrāyam.*

Bhishma [*bhīṣhma*]
The patriarch of both the Kaurava and Pandava families, whose story is told in the *Mahābhārata*; one of the great exemplars of piety, righteousness, kingship, and fortitude in that epic.

Blue Pearl [*nīla bindu*]
A brilliant blue light, the size of a tiny seed, which is the subtle abode of the Self; it appears to the meditator whose energy has been awakened by the grace of the Guru.

Brahma [*brahma*]
The supreme Lord in Vedic terminology; in the Hindu trinity of Brahma, Vishnu, and Shiva, the aspect of God as creator of the universe.

Brahman [*brahman*]
(*lit.* expansion; swelling of spirit) Vedantic term for the Absolute Reality.

Brahmin
Traditionally, the caste of priests and scholars.

Chidvilasananda, Swami [*Chidvilāsānanda*]
(*lit.* the bliss of the play of Consciousness) The name given to Gurumayi by Swami Muktananda when she took the vows of monkhood.

Consciousness
The intelligent, supremely independent, divine Energy that creates, pervades, and supports the entire universe.

Daivi sampatti [*daivī sampatti*]
(*lit.* divine wealth) The intrinsic virtues or strengths of the heart that, when honored and upheld, reveal the grace of God in one's seeking.

Darshan [*darśhan*]
(*lit.* viewing) Being in the presence of a great being; seeing God or an image of God.

Daya [*dayā*]
(*lit.* compassion) One of the magnificent virtues; the spiritual consciousness of another person's pain and a feeling of unselfish tenderness directed toward him without judgment or pity. *See also* karuna.

Dharana [*dhāraṇā*]
(*lit.* holding; bearing; keeping in remembrance) A technique for centering the mind and preparing it for meditation. In Patanjali's *Yoga Sūtras*, it is the sixth of the eight limbs of yoga.

Dharma [*dharma*]
Essential duty; the law of righteousness; living in accordance with the Divine Will. The highest dharma is to recognize the truth in one's own heart.

Dharmavyadha [*dharmavyādha*]
A great sage of Mithila who earned his livelihood as a simple butcher. His story appears in the *Mahābhārata.*

Drona [*droṇa*]
In the *Mahābhārata*, the great master of archery who taught the martial arts to both the Pandava and the Kaurava brothers when they were boys.

Ego
In yoga, the limited sense of "I" that is identified with the body, mind, and senses; sometimes described as "the veil of suffering."

Ganeshpuri [*gaṇeśhpurī*]
A village at the foot of the Mandagni Mountain in Maharashtra, India. Bhagawan Nityananda settled in this region where yogis have performed spiritual practices for thousands of years. Gurudev Siddha Peeth, the ashram that Baba Muktananda constructed at his Guru's command, is built on this sacred land. Gurumayi spent many of the years of her sadhana here. The Samadhi Shrines of Bhagawan Nityananda in Ganeshpuri and of Swami Muktananda at Gurudev Siddha Peeth attract many thousands of pilgrims.

Ganges
The most sacred river in India, the Ganges is said to originate in heaven. On earth, it flows down from the Himalayas, across all of North India, to the Bay of Bengal. It is believed that whoever bathes in the Ganges is purified of all sins.

Gunas [*guṇas*]
The three essential qualities of nature which determine the inherent characteristics of all created things. They are

sattva (purity, light, harmony, and intelligence); rajas (activity and passion); and tamas (dullness, inertia, and ignorance).

Guru [*guru*]
(*lit.* gu, darkness; ru, light) A spiritual teacher or Master who has attained oneness with God and who is therefore able both to initiate seekers and to guide them on the spiritual path to liberation. A Guru is also required to be learned in the scriptures and must belong to a lineage of Masters. *See also* Shaktipat; Siddha.

Guru's feet, Guru's sandals
The Guru's feet figure in most Indian scriptures, where they are said to embody Shiva and Shakti, knowledge and action, the emission and reabsorption of creation. Vibrations of the inner Shakti flow out from the Guru's feet. They are a mystical source of grace and illumination, and a figurative term for the Guru's teachings. This is why many beautiful and ancient hymns are addressed to them and to the Guru's sandals, which are also said to hold this divine energy of redemption and enlightenment.

Gurumayi [*Gurumāyī*]
(*lit.* one who is absorbed in the Guru) A term of respect and endearment in the Marathi language often used in addressing Swami Chidvilasananda.

Gurudev Siddha Peeth [*pīṭha*]
(Siddha peeth, *lit.* abode of perfected beings) The main ashram of Swami Chidvilasananda and of Siddha Yoga in Ganeshpuri, India. It is the site of the Samadhi Shrine of Baba Muktananda. Charged with the power of divine Consciousness, the ashram is a world-renowned center of spiritual practice and study.

Guru Gita [*guru gītā*]
(*lit.* the Song of the Guru) An ancient, sacred text; a garland of mantras that describe the nature of the Guru, the Guru-disciple relationship, and meditation on the Guru. In Siddha Yoga ashrams, the *Guru Gītā* is chanted every morning.

Guruseva
See seva.

Hanuman [*hanumān*]
(*lit.* heavy-jawed) A demigod in the form of a huge, white monkey who is one of the heroes of the *Rāmāyana*. Hanuman's unparalleled strength was exceeded only by his perfect devotion to Lord Rama, for whom he performed many acts of bravery and daring.

Hatha yoga
Yogic practices, both physical and mental, done for the purpose of purifying and strengthening both the physical and subtle bodies. *See also* yoga.

Indra, Lord [*indra*]
In the Vedas and Puranas, the lord of the heavens; the god of thunder and lightning.

Intensive
A program designed by Baba Muktananda to give direct initiation into the experience of meditation through the awakening of the Kundalini energy. *See also* Shaktipat.

Japa [*japa*]
(*lit.* prayer uttered in a low voice) Repetition of the mantra, either silently or aloud.

Jnana [*jñāna*]
(*lit.* high knowledge) Spiritual wisdom.

Jnana-vyavasthiti [*jñāna-vyavasthiti*]
(*lit.* steadfastness in knowledge) The divine quality of wholehearted dedication to knowledge, a state of virtue in which one is fixed on the truth of the Self and cannot be distracted.

Jnaneshwari [*jñāneśhwarī*]
A majestic commentary in verse on the *Bhagavad Gītā*, written by Jnaneshwar when he was sixteen, also known as the *Bhavarthadīpika*, "The Lamp of Simple Explanation." It was the first original scriptural work written in Marathi, the language of the people of Maharashtra. Composed "with the complete freedom of divine inspiration," as Baba Muktananda once said, it is a work of both great poetry and transforming spiritual insight. *See also* Jnaneshwar Maharaj.

Jnaneshwar Maharaj [*jñāneśhwar mahārāj*]
(ca. 1275-1296) Foremost among the poet-saints of Maharashtra, India, he was born into a family of saints. His elder brother Nivrittinath was his Guru; his younger brother, Sopan, and sister, Muktabai, also attained enlightenment in childhood. At the age of 21, Jnaneshwar took live samadhi (a yogi's voluntary departure from the body) in Alandi, where his samadhi shrine continues to attract thousands of seekers each year.

Kabir [*kabīr*]
(1440-1518) A great poet-saint and mystic who lived his life as a simple weaver in Benares. His followers included both Hindus and Muslims, and his influence was a powerful force in overcoming the fierce religious factionalism of the day. Bracing and penetrating, ecstatic and sobering, his poems describe the experience of the Self, the greatness of the Guru, and the nature of true spirituality. They are still being studied and sung all over the world.

Karma [*karma*]
(*lit.* action) The consequences of our verbal, mental, or physical actions, out of which our destiny is made. There are three categories of karma: that destined to be played out in this lifetime; that which is reserved for future lives, currently stored in seed form; and the karma being created in the present lifetime. *See also* samskaras.

Karmashaya [*karmāśhaya*]
(*lit.* reservoir of karmas) Accumulated impressions; the consequences of actions that are carried in one's being as imminent or future expressions of destiny.

Karna [*karṇa*]
Eldest brother of the Pandava princes. Not knowing his true ancestry, this great warrior took refuge with the wicked Kauravas and fought against his real brothers.

Karuna [*karūṇa*]
(*lit.* compassion; the mercy of God) A divine quality or virtuous state of forgiveness, empathy, and compassion, without attachment or ulterior motive.

Kashmir Shaivism
The sublime philosophy of nondualism that recognizes the entire universe as a manifestation of the one divine conscious energy; a branch of the Shaivite philosophical tradition that explains how the formless supreme Principle, Shiva, manifests as the universe. Together with Vedanta, Kashmir Shaivism

provides the basic scriptural context for Siddha Yoga.

Kauravas [*kauravas*]
Descendants of King Kuru, led by the wicked Duryodhana, who fought against the righteous Pandavas at the battle of Kurukshetra in the *Mahābhārata*.

Krishna [*kṛishṇa*]
(*lit.* the dark one; the one who attracts irresistibly) The eighth incarnation of Lord Vishnu, whose life story is described in the *Shrīmad Bhāgavatam* and the *Mahābhārata*, and whose spiritual teachings, as related to Arjuna on the battlefield, are known as the *Bhagavad Gītā*.

Krishnasuta [*kṛishṇasutā*]
(late 19th-early 20th century) Originally named Khado Krishna Garde. An educational inspector in the state of Karnataka, he was a follower of Siddharudha Swami in whose ashram Swami Muktananda took the vows of monkhood. Krishnasuta was the author of the *Gītāmrita Shatapadi*, 100 songs in the Marathi language summarizing the *Bhagavad Gītā*.

Kundalini [*kuṇḍalinī*]
(*lit.* coiled one) The supreme power or primordial energy that lies coiled at the base of the spine, in a dormant state, in every human being. When awakened, this extremely subtle force travels upward through the many channels of the subtle body, initiating various yogic practices and purifying the entire system. When purification is complete, Kundalini becomes established in the sahasrara, the spiritual center in the crown of the head. There the individual self merges into the supreme Self, and the cycle of birth and death comes to an end. *See also* Shaktipat.

Kuntibhoja [*kuntibhoja*]
In the *Mahābhārata*, the father of Kunti, who is the mother of the Pandavas.

Mahabharata [*mahābhārata*]
The great epic poem in Sanskrit, composed by the sage Vyasa, which recounts the struggle between the Kaurava and Pandava brothers over a disputed kingdom. Within this vast narrative is contained a wealth of Indian secular and religious lore. The *Bhagavad Gītā* occurs in the latter portion of the *Mahābhārata*.

Maharashtra [*mahārāśhtra*]
(*lit.* the great country) A state on the west coast of central India. Many of the great poet-saints lived in Maharashtra, and the Samadhi Shrines of Bhagawan Nityananda and Swami Muktananda are there. *See also* Ganeshpuri.

Mahavakya [*mahāvākya*]
(*lit.* great statements) Four statements containing the wisdom of the Upanishads, asserting the oneness of the individual Self and God: *aham brahmāsmi* (*Yajur Veda*); *ayam ātmā brahma* (*Atharva Veda*); *prajñānaṃ brahma* (*Rig Veda*); *tat tvam asi* (*Sāma Veda*).

Mala [*mala*]
(*lit.* impurity) A term used in Kashmir Shaivism to mean impurity, taint, dross; the misunderstanding of our nature that conceals and limits the pure power of divine Consciousness within us; the three limiting conditions that hamper the free expression of the spirit in a human being.

Mantra [*mantra*]
(*lit.* sacred invocation; that which protects) Mantras are the names of God; divine sounds invested with the power to

protect, purify, and transform the one who repeats them.

Matrika Shakti [*mātṛikā*]

(*lit.* power of the Mother) The Mother Goddess or Shakti, in the form of sound, as the creative force of the universe; the power of letters and words. *See also* Shakti.

Muktananda Paramahamsa, [*Muktānanda paramahaṃsa*] Swami

(1908-1982) Gurumayi's Guru, often referred to as Baba. This great Siddha brought the powerful and rare initiation known as shaktipat to the West on the command of his own Guru, Bhagawan Nityananda. As the inheritor of a great lineage of spiritual Masters, he introduced the path of Siddha Yoga all over the world, creating what he called a "meditation revolution." Baba made the scriptures come alive, teaching in words and action, by example and by direct experience. His message to everyone was: Honor your Self, worship your Self, meditate on your Self. Your God dwells within you as you.

Nadis [*nāḍīs*]

The 720 million channels in the subtle body of a human being through which the vital force circulates. The hubs or junction points of these nadis are known as the chakras.

Nityananda, Bhagawan [*Nityānanda*]

(?-1961) Swami Muktananda's Guru, also known as Bade Baba. He was a born Siddha, living his entire life in the highest state of Consciousness. Little is known of his early life. He came from South India and later lived in Maharashtra, where the village of Ganeshpuri grew up around him. He spoke very little, yet thousands of people experienced his grace. His Samadhi Shrine is located in the village of Ganeshpuri, a mile from Gurudev Siddha Peeth, the principal ashram of Siddha Yoga.

Om shantih shantih shantih [*śhāntiḥ*]

(Shanti, *lit.* peace) A prayer of peace and protection heralded by the primordial sound, *Om,* and offered at the end of Vedic prayers and hymns.

Paduka Arati [*pādukā āratī*]

The chant that accompanies morning and evening worship at the shrine of the great Siddha Sai Baba of Shirdi.

Panchatantra [*pañchatantra*]

Ancient teaching tales by the scholar Vishnu Sharma. Philosophy, morals and statecraft are taught through the mouths of animals and everyday characters and their exploits.

Pandavas [*pāṇḍava*s]

The sons of Pandu; the five virtuous heroes of the *Mahābhārata*, the great epic of India, who fought against the Kauravas in the battle for righteousness. These five brothers are named Yudhishthira, Bhima, Arjuna, Sahadev, and Nakula.

Parashiva [*paraśhiva*]

(*lit.* supreme Shiva) The primal Lord; the supreme Guru.

Prahva [*prahva*]

(*lit.* bowing before; humble) Humility; the tender virtue through which grace is absorbed, and by which all other virtues are nourished and ripened.

Prana [*prāṇa*]

The vital life-sustaining force of both the individual body and the entire universe.

Prashraya [*praśhraya*]
(*lit.* deferential respect) The reverence with which one offers respect to the supreme Self and calls upon grace, often in the form of invocation and prayer. Also, respect for the Self dwelling within all created things, sentient and insentient; a form of respect that is the basis of love.

Purandardas [*purandardās*]
(1484-1564) A wandering renunciant and Siddha who is looked upon as the father of Karnatic music; he expressed his devotion to Vitthal, a form of Vishnu, in every kind of composition from formal raga to lullaby. These songs, in the Kannada language, which have been hailed as the *Purandaropanishad*, are still being sung.

Rajas, rajoguna
See gunas.

Ramayana [*rāmāyaṇa*]
Attributed to the sage Valmiki, and one of the great epic poems of India. The *Rāmāyana* recounts the life and exploits of Lord Rama, the seventh incarnation of Vishnu. This story, so rich with spiritual meaning, has been told and retold down through the ages by saints, poets, scholars, and common folk.

Rasa [*rasa*]
Nectar, flavor; a subtle energy of richness, sweetness, and delight.

Rig Veda [*ṛig veda*]
One of the four Vedas, the *Rig Veda* is composed of over one thousand hymns of wisdom, containing some of the world's greatest poetry; this Veda is intended for the priest whose function is to recite the hymns inviting the gods to the fire rituals. *See also* Vedas.

Rumi, Jalaluddin
(1207-1273) The most eminent Sufi poet-saint of Persia and Turkey, and one of the greatest spiritual poets of all times. After meeting Shams-i Tabriz, an ecstatic wandering saint, he was transformed from a sober young scholar into an intoxicated singer of divine love.

Sadgurunath Maharaj ki Jay!
[*sadgurunāth mahārāj ki jaya!*]
(*lit.* I hail the Master who has revealed the Truth to me) An exalted, joyful expression of gratitude to the Guru for all that has been received.

Sadhana [*sādhana*]
Practices, both physical and mental, on the spiritual path; spiritual discipline.

Sadhu [*sādhu*]
A holy being, monk, or ascetic.

Sahaja Samadhi [*sahaja samādhi*]
The natural state of meditative union with the Absolute, which remains continuous throughout the waking, dream and deep sleep states.

Sahasrara [*sahasrāra*]
The thousand-petaled spiritual center at the crown of the head, where one experiences the highest states of consciousness. *See also* nadis.

Samadhi Shrine [*samādhi*]
Final resting place of a great yogi's body. Such shrines are places of worship, alive with their spiritual power and blessings.

Sama Veda [*sāma veda*]
One of the four Vedas, the *Sāma Veda* is a liturgical collection of hymns sung to melodies of great beauty. *See also* Vedas.

Samskaras [*saṃskāras*]
Impressions of past actions and thoughts that remain in the subtle body. They are brought to the surface of one's awareness and then eliminated by the action of the awakened Kundalini energy. *See also* karma.

Sannyasa [*sannyāsa*]
Monkhood; the ceremony and vows in which one renounces the responsibilities and privileges of worldly life and dedicates oneself exclusively to the goal of Self-realization and service to God; in India, traditionally, the final stage of life, which occurs after all worldly obligations have been fulfilled.

Sanskrit [*saṇskṛit*]
(*lit.* complete) The language of the ancient Indian texts.

Saptah [*saptah*]
(*lit.* seven days, from ancient tradition of seven-day chants) The continuous chanting of the name of God which may be accompanied by dancing in a circle in a series of measured steps as an act of devotion and a kinetic form of meditation.

Satsang [*satsaṅga*]
(*lit.* the company of the Truth) The company of saints and devotees; a gathering of devotees for the purpose of chanting, meditating, and listening to scriptural teachings or readings.

Sattva guna
See gunas.

Sattva-samshuddhi [*sattva-saṃśhuddhi*]
(*lit.* purity of being) One of the magnificent virtues; more than just cleansing the mind, strengthening the intellect, and purifying the body, sattva-samshuddhi means becoming completely established in the absolute purity of the essence of one's being; a state that evolves out of pure actions.

Self
The atman, or divine Consciousness residing in the individual; described as the witness of the mind, or the pure I-awareness.

Self-inquiry
The process of contemplating the questions "Who am I? What am I? Where have I come from?" and "What is the purpose of my life?" The practice of self-inquiry strips away illusion, bringing one closer and closer to the experience of the Self within.

Seva [*sevā*]
(*lit.* service) Selfless service; work offered to God, performed with an attitude of nondoership and without attachment.

Shaivism
See Kashmir Shaivism.

Shakti [*śhakti*]
Spiritual power; grace. The divine cosmic power that creates and maintains the universe. The dynamic aspect of supreme Consciousness. *See also* Kundalini.

Shaktipat [*śhaktipāta*]
(*lit.* the descent of grace) The transmission of spiritual power (Shakti) from the Guru to the disciple; spiritual awakening. *See also* Kundalini.

Shankaracharya [*śhaṅkarāchārya*]
(780-820) One of the greatest philosophers and sages of all time. He spread the philosophy of absolute nondualism (Advaita Vedanta) throughout India. In addition to

teaching and writing, he established ashrams in the four corners of the country. The tradition of monks to which Swami Chidvilasananda and Swami Muktananda belong was created by Shankaracharya. One of his famous works is the *Viveka Chūḍāmaṇi*, "The Crest Jewel of Discrimination."

Sheikh Nasruddin

A legendary figure originating in Turkish folklore during the Middle Ages, used by teachers in many parts of the world to illustrate the antics of the human mind.

Shirdi Sai Baba [*śhirḍī sāī bābā*]

(1838-1918) One of the great Siddhas of modern times. Although he spent his entire life in a small country town, he became known all over India. Just before leaving his body, he said, "Now the stones of this samadhi will answer your prayers." His powerful samadhi shrine at Shirdi, in central Maharashtra, is a popular place of pilgrimage.

Shiva [*śhiva*]

In Kashmir Shaivism, the Self of all; the all-pervasive, unchanging, transcendent Consciousness; in the Hindu trinity of Brahma, the creator, and Vishnu, the sustainer, Shiva is the third aspect of God, the destroyer of ignorance.

Shivo'ham [*śhivo'ham*]

(*lit.* I am Shiva) An ancient mantra that proclaims one's own inner Self as the Supreme Reality.

Shloka [*śhloka*]

A verse, in Sanskrit, from a spiritual text or scripture.

Siddha [*siddha*]

A perfected yogi; one who lives in the state of unity-consciousness and who has achieved mastery over the senses and their objects; one whose experience of the supreme Self is uninterrupted and whose identification with the ego has been broken.

Siddha Yoga

The spiritual path to union of the individual and the divine, which begins with shaktipat, the initiation given by the grace of a Siddha Guru. Siddha Yoga is also known as Maha Yoga, "the great yoga," because it includes all other branches of yoga. Swami Chidvilasananda, Swami Muktananda's successor, is the living Master of this ancient path.

Six enemies

The inner enemies spoken about in Vedanta: desire, anger, delusion, pride, greed, and envy.

Skanda Purana [*skanda purāṇa*]

One of eighteen major sacred books of Hindu legends and hymns about the gods and the sages, which were compiled by the sage Vyasa.

So'ham [*so'ham*]

(*lit.* That I am) The natural vibration of the Self, which occurs spontaneously with each incoming and outgoing breath. By becoming completely aware of this mantra, which is constantly repeating inside us, a seeker is able to experience oneness with the supreme Self.

South Fallsburg, New York

The location of the Siddha Yoga meditation ashram which Baba Muktananda established as international headquarters of the SYDA Foundation in 1979.

Spanda Karikas [*spanda kārikās*]

One of the fundamental scriptures of Kashmir Shaivism; this 9th century collection of 53 verses composed by Vasuguptacharya describes how the yogi who remains alert can perceive the divine vibration, or spanda, in all of life.

Sushumna [*suṣhumnā*]
The central and most important channel (nadi) of the subtle body, it extends from the base of the spine to the top of the head; the purifying Kundalini energy (Shakti) rises within it to pierce the seven spiritual centers known as chakras. *See also* Kundalini; nadis.

Svatantrya [*svātantrya*]
The absolute innate freedom and boundless spontaneity of the Lord.

Swami *or* Swamiji [*swāmi*]
A respectful term of address for a sannyasin or monk.

Tadasana [*tāḍāsana*]
The hatha yoga posture in which one stands firm and tall like a mountain.

Tagore, Rabindranath
(1861-1941) The Nobel prizewinning Bengali poet, educator, and visionary, whose work helped to introduce Indian culture to the West.

Tamas, tamoguna
See gunas.

Tao Te Ching
(*lit.* The Way and Its Power) The classic scripture of Taoism by Lao Tsu, which holds that there is a basic principle of harmony in the universe, known as the Tao.

Tapasya [*tapasya*]
(*lit.* heat) Austerities; the experience of heat that occurs during the process of practicing yoga. This heat is generated by friction between the mind and the heart, between the demand of the senses and the impulse of renunciation. It is said that this heat, "the fire of yoga," burns up all the impurities that lie between the seeker and the experience of the Truth.

Tulsidas [*tulsīdāsa*]
(1532-1623) The poet-saint of North India who wrote in Hindi the *Rāma Charitamānasa*, the life story of Rama, still one of the most popular scriptures in India today.

Upadesha [*upadeśha*]
(*lit.* to sit near the Truth) Spiritual instruction, teachings that carry the power of initiation.

Upanishads [*upaniṣhads*]
(*lit.* sitting close to; secret teachings) The inspired teachings, visions, and mystical experiences of the ancient sages, rishis, of India. These scriptures, exceeding 100 texts, constitute "the end" or "final understanding" (anta) of the Vedas; hence the term Vedanta. With immense variety of form and style, all of these texts give the same essential teaching, that the individual soul and God are one.

Vasishtha [*vāsiṣhṭha*]
The legendary sage and Guru of Lord Rama. Vasishtha epitomized the force of spiritual knowledge. He is the central figure of the *Yoga Vāsishtha*, which is one of the most rigorous scriptures on the nature of the mind and the way to free it from illusion.

Vedanta [*vedānta*]
(*lit.* end of the Vedas) One of the six orthodox schools of Indian philosophy, exemplified by the Upanishads and other texts that consider the nature of the Self.

Vedas [*vedas*]
(*lit.* knowledge) Among the most ancient, revered, and sacred of the world's scriptures, the four Vedas are regarded as divinely revealed, eternal wisdom. They are *Rig Veda*, *Atharva Veda*, *Sāma Veda*, and *Yajur Veda*.

Vedic fire ceremony
Known as *yajna*. A sacred fire ritual lasting several days. Vedic mantras are recited while items such as fragrant woods, grains, and ghee are poured into the fire as an offering to the Lord, and as gratitude for all we have received.

Viveka [*viveka*]
(*lit.* discrimination; distinction) The faculty of discretion that enables a human being to distinguish between true and false, reality and illusion.

Viveka Chudamani [*viveka chūḍāmaṇi*]
(*lit.* The Crest Jewel of Discrimination) An 8th-century philosophical Sanskrit commentary on Advaita Vedanta written by Shankaracharya, it expounds the teaching that Brahman, the Absolute, alone is real. It is considered to be a prime example of the philosophical genius, as well as the spiritual attainment, of this great Siddha Master.

Yajur Veda [*yajur veda*]
An eternal scripture whose hymns specify sacrificial formulas and rites and the rules for their correct performance, which are said to control the harmonious functioning of the universe.

Yoga [*yoga*]
(*lit.* union) The spiritual practices and disciplines that lead a seeker to evenness of mind, to the severing of the union with pain and, through nondoership, to skill in action; ultimately the path of yoga leads to the experience of the Self.

Yoga Sutras of Patanjali [*Patañjali Yoga Sūtras*]
A collection of aphorisms written in Sanskrit in the 4th century by the sage Patanjali. This is the basic scripture of the eight limbs of the path of yoga. It expounds the different methods for the attainment of samadhi.

Yoga Vasishtha [*yoga vāsiṣhṭha*]
Also known as *Vāsishtha Rāmāyana*. A very popular Sanskrit text on Advaita Vedanta, probably written in the 12th century, and ascribed to the sage Valmiki. In it, Vasishtha answers Lord Rama's philosophical questions on life, death, and human suffering by teaching that the world is as you see it and that illusion ceases when the mind is stilled.

Yoga-vyavasthiti [*yoga-vyavasthiti*]
(*lit.* steadfastness in yoga) One of the magnificent virtues mentioned by Lord Krishna in chapter sixteen of the *Bhagavad Gītā*; the ability of a seeker to practice yoga, come what may, with determination and an undismayed mind; the ability to sustain the prolonged endeavor of the spiritual path.

INDEX

Further Reading

BY SWAMI MUKTANANDA

Play of Consciousness: A Spiritual Autobiography

From the Finite to the Infinite

I Have Become Alive

The Perfect Relationship

Reflections of the Self

Secret of the Siddhas

I Am That

Kundalini

Mystery of the Mind

Does Death Really Exist?

Light on the Path

Mukteshwari

Bhagawan Nityananda of Ganeshpuri

Meditate

Nothing Exists That Is Not Shiva

BY SWAMI CHIDVILASANANDA

Kindle My Heart

Pulsation of Love

Courage and Contentment

The Yoga of Discipline

Smile, Smile, Smile!

Enthusiasm

Inner Treasures

The Magic of the Heart

Remembrance

You can learn more about the teachings and practices of Siddha Yoga meditation by contacting:

SYDA Foundation
371 Brickman Road, P.O. Box 600,
South Fallsburg, NY 12779-0600, USA
(845) 434-2000

or

Gurudev Siddha Peeth
P.O. Ganeshpuri
PIN 401 206
District Thana
Maharashtra, India

For further information about books in print by Swami Chidvilasananda and Swami Muktananda, and editions in translation, please contact:

Siddha Yoga Bookstore
371 Brickman Road, P.O.Box 600,
South Fallsburg, NY 12779-0600, USA
Tel: (845) 434-2000 ext. 1700